Acknowledgement

The Friends of
Montague Rotary Library
have generously provided
financial assistance
for the publishing of this
2014 project.

The Montague Library
Writers Guild wishes
to extend its sincere gratitude to
the Friends of Montague
Rotary Library
for this much appreciated
help to make the publishing
of our book
"VOICES" possible.

Prince Edward Island Voices

Copyright 2014. by the respective writers and photographers. All rights reserved. No part of this book may be used in any form or by any means "graphical, electronic, or mechanical" without written permission of the copyright owners. Purchase and author-contact information is available from the publisher:

    Wood Island Prints
    670 Trans-Canada Highway, RR 1
    Belle River, PE C0A 1B0
    (902) 962-3335 schultz@pei.sympatico.ca
    www.woodislandsprints.com

For information about the Writers Guild you may contact:
    Montague Rotary Library
    Montague, PE C0A 1R0
    (902) 838-2928 montague.gov.pe.ca

Contact the printer at:
    Lightning Source Inc.
    1246 Heil Quaker Blvd.
    La Vergne, TN 37086 USA
    Voice: (615) 213-5815
    Fax: (615) 213-4725
    Email: inquiry@lightningsource.com
    www.lightningsource.com

ISBN 978-0-9918033-8-5

Second printing (with spelling and punctuation corrections)

Introduction

On behalf of the Montague Library Writers Guild, its members and especially the writers of works contained in this book, I extend a very warm welcome.

We are a group of over fifty writers. We have grown and come together during the past five years for various reasons, but mainly, to share our love of writing and to learn through that sharing.

This book began several months ago as a group writing project. Like our previous two compilations, it has helped us experience, first hand, the joy of transferring thoughts of mind and feelings of heart to written word. At the same time, we hope it helps you to see why we are so passionate about our Island home. This book features an eclectic selection of prose and poetry, most focused on this place we love.

Individually, we have published fourteen other books, in hard- and soft-cover, and eBook formats. Topics are as varied as our members.

We would like to dedicate VOICES to Swarna Chandrasekera, librarian at the Montague Rotary Library. It was Swarna's vision that brought us together at the library.

We invite you now, to turn the page, listen to our voices, and begin your journey to a place that is very special, to all of us.

Gary Gray
Chair

Table of Contents

Doreen Bears 1
    The Little Firefighter 1947 2
    My Little Piece of Heaven 5

Jeannee Bradley 9
    Cars 11
    Home Deliveries 13
    A Memory of a Child 15
    Ice Racing in Charlottetown 16
    First Impression 17
    An Unexpected Message 18

James Bruce 19
    Island Reflections 20
    Technical Terms 24
    The Battle of Creed's Pond 25

John Burck 29
    The Crash of Argus Aircraft 737 31
    A Believable FERRY Tale 38
    The Stuff of Legends 41

Gary Gray 45
    Yellow School 46
    Gray's Transport 49
    Blue Bicycle 53

Terry Kerr 55
    Celebrate Winter! 56
    The Ocean 57
    The Deadly Storm 58
    Island Healing 61

Sheila Mallory 63
    The Sparrow 65
    Murray Harbour 67

Joanne Collicott McGuigan 71
    The Tragedy of Minnie McGee 72

Blanche Moyaert 87
    Becoming an Islander 87

Nancy Perkins 105
    The Gosh Darn Plow 106
    The Ice Floe 108

Table of Contents

    Nature Lovers 109
    The Blue Jar 110
    Island Blue 111
    The Astronaut Visit 112
    Booms in Little Sands 114

Tom Rath 115
    Connections 116
    Unexpected Dinner Guest 117
    Visitors are Surprised 118
    Don't 'Stop Playing With Your Food!' 120
    Winter Whirl 121
    Fur-Children 122

Tom Schultz 123
    Winter Night Drive Home 124
    Winter Night Sounds 126
    Island Funerals 129

Donna Singleton 133
    February 14th 1967 134
    Russell (A Good Old Boy) 140

Kim Smith 145
    PEI Has Only Three Seasons 146
    An Island Reverie 147
    Winter Storms 148
    If You Need Any Help Just Call! 150

Karen Stewart 153
    My Eureka Moments 154

Linda Stewart 163
    Downsized 165
    This Place 166
    Watercolour Pastels 167
    Light and Stardust 168
    My Island 169
    The Farmers Market 170
    Farm Living 172
    A Memorable Meal 173
    Perfect Silence 174
    God Sounds 174

Doreen Bears

I was born and raised in Sydney, Nova Scotia but have spent three-quarters of my life here on Prince Edward Island. Education has been an ongoing process for a few years from high-school graduation at Holy Redeemer Convent to University of Toronto then to UPEI and finally the PEI School of Nursing.

Writing poems and short stories began in grade school but along the way, it was put on a back burner to pursue all the other wonderful challenges life had to offer.

My passions are many. Music, theatre, painting, reading and writing, to name a few. However, and most importantly my wonderful husband of forty-eight years, my three fantastic children, their spouses, my six grandsons and one granddaughter. They are my greatest passion. Last but not least, my old and new friends who have been there for me on this wonderful challenging roller coaster ride over the years.

The Little Firefighter 1947

Back in 1947 Belle River had its youngest firefighter, a four year old boy. This little boy lived in a modest three-bedroom, two-story wood house with all the necessities. An Enterprise stove burned wood and kerosene lamps were the source of heat and light. A hand pump was the source of water with an icebox and later on a kerosene refrigerator. An outhouse in all its elegance stood approximately one hundred feet from the main house. There was a workshop, garage and a hen house which housed about a hundred hens.

Doreen Bears: The Little Firefighter 1947

Across the shore road were eight cows, a pig and a huge garden. Life was good. The mother and father worked the small farm and at times the father was on the road trucking for the extra income.

Young Danny was too young to officially attend school on a regular basis but the teacher, Joyce MacLennan, would allow him to come to school whenever he was bored at home. He had a trike with a wooden seat which his father had made and he would bike the quarter mile trip to school whenever he wanted.

One day he looked out the school window and saw smoke and fire billowing into the sky from the direction of his grandfather's farm. He hopped on his trike and hurried home to fetch a dipper of water to help put out the blaze.

Most fires back in those days were usually caused by lightning. This was harvest time and the fire broke out during the process of threshing sheaves of grain in the mill. After the grain was separated the straw was then put through a chopper blower and blown into a loft all in one motion. In this case, some straw wound up in the shaft of the blower and that created sparks which blew into the loft. Dried straw and dust was the perfect combination to start a fire.

VOICES

Young Danny knew that time was of great importance here and he had to hurry with his dipper of water to help out. He raced on his trike frantically along the dirt road not realizing that the water was spilling all over his legs.

In those days there were no fire stations. They used a gasoline powered pump with a long canvas hose. The pump forced the water from the river into this canvas hose, which was very dry and leaked profusely from not being used frequently. By the time the leaking stopped, it was too late. The fire was raging out of control. Young Danny arrived with an empty dipper and he was devastated. He watched people running in all directions trying to do something to help out. His Uncle Hector lived close by so he pedalled over there to watch the big barn burn to the ground.

(To supply names: The little boy was John Daniel Bears, son of Benjamin and Maud Bears. The teacher was Joyce MacLennan, and the barn belonged to Jack Compton.)

Doreen Bears: My Little Piece of Heaven

My Little Piece of Heaven

For a short while each year the beach in front of my home on the Northumberland Strait belongs only to me. After the summer folks return to their winter homes and the tourists have finished their vacations it becomes my little piece of heaven.

It is a September evening, still quite warm and sunny. I walk across my lawn to a small staircase leading down to the beach. On my right, to the west, the sun with all of its brilliance and heavenly colour is just setting. I can venture quite a distance from shore when the tide is out. I am the only human presence on the beach but soon the sandpipers frolic around my feet, a pair of Canada geese flies overhead and the ever-persistent black raven with its aggravating cawing demands its share of the beach. The gulls in their many different species are always present. Tiny fish break water in the falling tide. The birds are after their supper, the swallows dart in and out of their little holes along the cliff. Each bird has a different melody and all contribute to a wonderful oceanside symphony.

I come closer to the Point, where the sand runs into a pile of huge rocks and a family of seals sunbathe every day. This evening the only onlooker is me and they are starting to congregate in large

numbers. Somehow they know I am not a threat to them. At times I will swim as close as five feet away from them. They are so curious and they actually play the *hen-rooster-chicken-duck* game we all played with our children in the water. They have the most beautiful trusting eyes and are ever so playful. When they talk with each other, they bark and also howl like a wolves. It's a very eerie sound. When I try to imitate them I'm sure they are wondering what species I belong to.

Suddenly, I am startled by three blue herons ascending from behind the rocks. I must have disturbed them. They appear gigantic and so majestic with their six-foot wingspan. I marvel at the grace and gentleness of these huge birds as they take flight. For a few moments I sit on the rocks to absorb the tranquility and the beauty surrounding me. How much closer can one get to God or to Heaven?

The tide begins its journey back to shore. It is time to leave this place of peace. The sun is dipping below the horizon. It reminds me of pulling down my Venetian blinds. The birds have had their supper. The seals are still bathing in the twilight. They will keep vigilance throughout the night and their cries will become louder as dusk settles in. I am not sure if it is just a ritual or whether they really do keep watch. On my way back I observe the hermit crabs scooting across the sand. I think about their struggle to survive in this turbulent environment. I pick one up and immediately it retreats into its

shell. I want to know more about these tiny creatures. They will be a good study for the long winter months ahead.

As much as this walk on the beach lifts my spirits I sometimes feel a tinge of sadness. So many people in the world will never see what I see nor hear what I hear, as I walk and share this beach with so many wonderful creatures.

There is an old saying, "What you don't have you don't miss."

This gives me a little comfort for the selfish feeling that I have about owning this beautiful beach if only for a little while.

VOICES

Jeannee Bradley

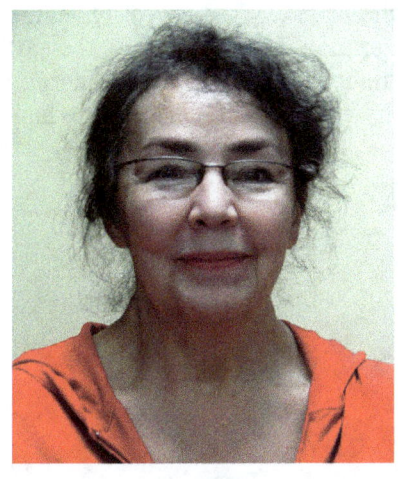

I was born in Charlottetown, PEI when the streets were clay and the sidewalks were wooden. Dogs and cats played outside as did children of every age. Girls went to one school and boys to another until high school and then you each used separate doors. Church was a very strong presence in the community and your week was planned by the activities at the church. The norm was Devotions on Tuesdays, Confession on Saturdays, Mass on Sundays and the Rosary every night before supper. I played, laughed and danced all through elementary, high school and university.

I married, had four children and was widowed at the age of thirty-five. I worked at a canteen in the summer for fun (and money) when I was twelve years old. I've always enjoyed the people I've met and worked with throughout the years at places like Rogers Hardware as a cashier, Bank of Montreal as a teller and supervisor, in Justice and Education as a Youth Worker and Life Skills Coach, and at Red Shores as a Banker and Customer Service Repersentative. Now I am writing Policy and Procedure Manuals for the Salvation Army and learning something new every day.

I've always wanted to keep a journal and couldn't seem to get started. I joined the Montague Library Writers Guild with a friend to try and get my thoughts on paper. So commenced my writing journey with the encouragement and support of the group.

In a month or two I will be eligible for my pension and hope to live for many more years so I can enjoy all of Prince Edward

VOICES

Island's many beauties and to experience the diversity that now exists in a community shared by those that have experienced war and the Depression, Baby Boomers who have worked for thirty years in one place and are proud of it, Generation X's who protects the earth and the environment and the extremely knowledgeable Generation Y's who can communicate with the entire world from a little hand-held device in a matter of seconds.

Cars

Today I got my car registered but before I could do that I had to have it inspected. On inspection it was suggested that it may be a good idea to get a new tire as I would *soon* be in need of one.

I thought, "OK, I guess they know what they are talking about."

I told them to proceed after I got an estimate. The estimate included a price for *two tires* which they explained, "It's advisable to get two tires to keep the car balanced." While installing the tires they observed that the caliper on the left would *soon* need work (I'm guessing they knew what they were talking about) and after an estimate, which came back with the price for *two* calipers (because they said, it was best to keep the car balanced) I told them to proceed. Seven hundred and some dollars later, my 2009 car was ready. Now I could pay approximately a hundred dollars to get it registered. There at Access PEI they told me that I also needed a new license plate for another five dollars.

I remember a car my brother's friend bought when he was fourteen years old. He hid it around the corner from his place so his father wouldn't know he had it. The first day the guys on the corner drove in it for a long time, then decided to add some gas to it. Much to their surprise the station attendant informed them the car had no gas tank. There was only a hose that led into the trunk and into a glass bottle.

One of my brothers had a red Cougar that one of my sisters gave to him. It wasn't long before his two-year-old daughter lost the keys while 'playing car'. Forever after that the car was 'hotwired' and life went on as normal.

It was the custom for my older sisters to pass down their cars, so my next brother got my next sister's Chevy. It was a huge car that my brother called 'Silvio'. It lasted for quite a while. It did, however, eventually have trouble with the passenger side door. The hinge was loose or something so my brother would open the passenger side door by unravelling a big rope from his inside handle just enough for a passenger to get in. Then he would wind it up again to close the door. No problem.

My boyfriend, whom I eventually married, bought a 1950 Chevy that he put in my father's barn. He covered the car windows with newspaper and spray-painted the car a forest green. It had the most comfortable seats I have ever experienced. Back then they were like a couch. The only glitch with the car was that he had to run beside it for a few minutes to get it started (that's called 'jump starting'). He was young and in good shape and he happily did this for a long time.

After my husband died, I could not let go of the last car we owned together, so I pretty well drove it into the ground and very unwillingly allowed it to limp painfully out of my life. After a while it was obvious I needed transportation as I had three active children. This would be my first major purchase without my husband and I wanted to do it on my own. I found a car for sale that was in the country. A male friend of the family came with me for support. As I drove up to the farm, I saw a glistening burgundy car sitting in the sunshine, just as though it was waiting for me. The owner came out to meet me and we walked into the field. As we got closer to the car the gleam kind of turned into a haze. I thought that with a little elbow grease the shine would surely come back. It never did. In the meantime my friend kept shaking his head slowly from side to side with a deer-caught-in-the-headlight look. I chalked it up to, "What a find!".

There was a little trouble getting it started, which I could understand. It had been sitting for quite awhile, apparently, in the field in the sun and it needed some urging along. The owner pumped it three times, turned the key, pumped it three times again, turned the key, then once more pumped it three times and turned the key all to no avail. So he got out of the car and chatted for a while with me. Our family friend seemed quite tongued-tied or shy or something for he was still just shaking his head from side to side, side to side.

Finally it started. I jumped in and I drove slowly, *tediously, painstakingly* and finally got it home. I guess that a few months without a car made me rusty. Our friend followed me home, kind of waved, then looked straight ahead and drove away. I don't remember if I ever saw him again. My mom was excited for me but everyone else sort of looked like the family friend did when they saw my purchase.

I do have to admit that this car had some personal issues and a mind of its own. Quite often on a drive it would just slow down on its own. No amount of pumping the gas pedal would egg it on. Then all of a sudden it would take off like a bat out Halifax. You had to be on the alert at all times with this buggy. It also developed a bit of a quirk and then you had to tap something under the hood. My children, much to my chagrin, could manage this but I couldn't quite find the right spot. So I just tapped everything. The hood, the sides and even the license plate until eventually the car would start. I have very vague memories of what actually happened to this car in the end, but my younger brother gave me a deal so I could have his nice, really shiny, black Cavalier.

I notice, sadly, that no one seems to give their cars names anymore. In any case, I guess the streets are safer now and the motor vehicle department is making lots of money for the province, but I sure miss seeing cars with character.

Home Deliveries

I was quite perturbed by the announcement that the postal service may eliminate home mail delivery. Not that Canada Post would ever be able to survive with my purchases but nonetheless it really affected me.

It reminds me of all the vendors that came to the front door of my home in Charlottetown all the years I was growing up.

We had a milkman, a mailman and an egg lady. We had 'Dan Dan' the honey man, and a man that came to sell his homemade whittled wooden clothes poles which were used to prop up clotheslines to prevent freshly washed clothes from sweeping the ground. My mom bought a new one every spring but sometimes had to buy one or two later as they often went missing. There was a guy from the town of Souris up on the northeastern tip of the Island who brought in salt cod and a farmer that regularly delivered vegetables. We also had a Watkins man, an iceman and a coalman. Each one of these deliveries consisted of a visit and an update on people's lives, their children and their animals. Tea was often made, sometimes even a snack, for these people were considered visitors and friends.

Bits of information were passed on through the years, such as the money from the eggs was the egg lady's own spending money which she relished being able to use.

Some deliveries were kind of mysterious. A small man in a grey top coat and a brown fedora would come to the house at dusk. Out from his inside coat pocket would appear a small piece of paper and my father would get some money from my mom and pass it to the man, all without much chatter. Then the man would slip out the door and disappear into a neighbour's house. Years later I found out he sold Irish Sweepstakes tickets. Apparently this was forbidden, but everyone seemed to buy them.

We had three papers delivered daily: *The Guardian, The Patriot* and *The Halifax Herald. The Post Call,* which was a paper dedicated to local horse racing and breeding, was also delivered weekly. We had regular mail from my sister who moved out West to teach and from my other two sisters who went to live in Ontario. My mom loved her visits with the Avon lady who would drop in with her goodies. The Eatons and Sears catalogues arrived seasonally. Mom did all this and still very calmly took care of a home, her husband, nine children, a few animals and her ageing parents. She loved the visits and so did the visitors. No one seemed rushed. Legs were crossed, tea was drunk and nods and laughter prevailed.

I know we still get flyers flung up the driveway and bills hand delivered to the door, but the idea of losing even that makes me nostalgic and sad.

A Memory of a Child

Torch is a man in his seventies and a regular at the Legion on Pownal Street in Charlottetown. He often stops there on his way home after getting groceries, having a shave and a haircut or picking up a newspaper.

If he happens upon you along his way, he will treat you to a beverage of your choice and reminisce about his childhood in particular when he was nine years old when he and his dad used to regularly visit the barns at the race track on Exhibition Drive in Charlottetown.

On one such occasion he heard my father speak of a horse that was racing the next day. Apparently my father had said that if it rained that such and such a horse would win as he was "good in the mud". As nature would have it, it did rain. When Torch and his dad approached the track he begged his father for two dollars.

"Why?" his dad asked. This was an unusual request from a son who usually just watched and listened.

"Dad, you have to. Tommy said this horse likes the mud. Please, Dad, please!"

So his father bought the ticket and the horse did come in, winning one hundred and sixty dollars. Excited and proud Torch was beaming.

On the way home, Torch got an ice cream cone at the service station. The rest went to buy clothes and supplies for school. To this very day, Torch still says that the money didn't matter. That the memory of that day is worth a million dollars!

VOICES

Ice Racing in Charlottetown

I remember the flurry of preparation when Daddie and the others got themselves, their horses and their gear ready for the big ice race down the main street in Charlottetown. The streets were lined with crowds of people anticipating the grand parade of dashing horses and the exciting outcome.

I was there on the corner of Queen and Richmond Street when the horses sped by with slush and snow flying from the wheels of the carts. People were screaming and cheering. Some of them shouting, "Go, Tommy, go!"

Then I saw my dad. "This must be what Thor the Thunder God looked like when he commanded the awe of those in his presence," I thought.

He was strong and vibrant and so confident of his ability and that of his mighty steed. I don't really remember if he won. I was told he did. It didn't really matter for he was the hero of my life then as always. He was the man against whom all others were to be measured. He didn't have to be on a horse in the middle of a cheering crowd. I felt the same when he quietly covered his horse with a blanket and walked him lovingly into the stall, then came in and sat with his family for supper and was there, ever-present, as his children went to bed.

First Impression

He often sat in the back of the blacksmith shop on Euston Street in Charlottetown when he took his horses there to be shod, quite content to share some bits of information with the local blacksmith, Mr. Moreside, as he worked.

The evening was quiet, only the steady sound of the hammer hitting the anvil permeated the air. Just then out of the corner of his eye he saw a shadow gliding toward the entrance to the shop.

To him she appeared as though she could be in a beauty soap advertisement. Her skin was smooth, flawless and a perfect setting for her large grey eyes and Mona Lisa smile.

She didn't hesitate to approach the huge animal before her. She merely nodded to the blacksmith, walked up to the horse and reached for the bridle that cupped his mouth. She stood on her tip toes and breathed gently into his nostrils.

The effect was relaxing to the large beast and exhilarating to her observer. She stayed for just a while, silent and unaware of her impact, then left as quietly as she had come. An oasis in a desert to a thirsty man. Elusive but unforgettable.

This is what my father saw the very first time he saw my mother.

VOICES

An Unexpected Message

I was at a function at the local Legion, when a man ten to fifteen years older than I was approached me and said, "You have to be..." and he used my maiden name. He too looked familiar to me from my childhood.

He smiled and seemed genuinely happy to talk to me. He said, "You know, I and many others owe a lot to your dad."

I'm sure I looked at him strangely for I didn't know what he meant. He continued, saying that as soon as it got dark out, he or his brothers - as many others did - were sent to my father's side yard to gather slabs of wood to burn in their wood stoves. Night after winter night this became a ritual. The slabs were always replaced the next day and awaited those that may need them the following night. Never a word was exchanged.

He grew quiet with a tenderness forming in his eyes. Then he said, "Your dad gave us warmth, but more so, dignity for those that didn't have the means to get what they needed sometimes."

The next day I asked my mother about this and she said that, yes, she had known. I asked why we did not know. She replied that there was no reason for anyone else to know.

My father owned a lumber mill near the corner of Queen and Connolly Street in Charlottetown and he felt that in no way should anyone be cold when he had wood that he could leave out, nor should they have to ask for it.

James Bruce

Born in Nova Scotia and raised in Montreal, Jim lived for many years in Toronto.

He worked in the creative side of the advertising business as an art director and copywriter and then began to work internationally as a creative director. He worked for many years in Mexico City as well as the Dominican Republic and Costa Rica. He worked for McCann Erickson for their offices in both Trinidad and Tobago and Barbados. He later worked for Ogilvy & Mather in their office in Kiev and lastly on Malta.

He moved to eastern PEI six years ago, perhaps for good. He speaks French and Spanish and currently teaches English and Spanish as a volunteer in Montague.

VOICES

Island Reflections

The move from downtown Toronto to rural eastern PEI was an experiment but after six months they agreed that it was working. As freelance French-to-English translators both of them with solid clients they found that they could easily work from home.

During their first weeks in the old farmhouse they had bought, the deep, velvety silence at night had been eerie. For suddenly ticking with an unbearable loudness they banished a clock from the bedroom to the living room. After two weeks they cancelled their subscription to the newspaper. The sound of the delivery car pulling up to their mailbox at the end of their lane in the pre-dawn hours woke them each day.

"You know, Lisa, I was thinking that we need a different car." Jeff said over breakfast early in June.

"Ok. What did you have in mind?"

"I was thinking about an SUV or a pick-up truck. Or," he mused, "a big Durango."

"Jeff, we moved here from Toronto not Alberta."

They bought a Jeep. Brilliantly new and gleaming black with four-wheel drive, GPS and very, very big tires. Lisa felt it was just too bulky and brawny-looking. Too brash for two people in their early forties (both with Master's degrees in Linguistics) but Jeff was in love with it so she went along.

"Lisa, can you come outside for a minute?"

"What is it, Jeff?"

"Would you *please* come outside?"

"She stepped out onto the side porch and found him standing in the drive with his back turned to her, hands on his hips, staring intently at the new Jeep.

"What is it?"

"Look at the side mirror here," he pointed without turning to her, "and the mirror on the other side."

She walked up to the vehicle and saw it. On the top of the otherwise immaculate black plastic cowlings of each side mirror were at least a dozen very small, but very deep, dents scattered across the surface.

"What's done this?" she asked, fingering the tiny little holes.

"When you last drove it didn't you hear any gravel pinging against the car?"

"When I last drove it? Why are you assuming this happened when I was driving?"

"Because I would have noticed if it had happened when I was driving and I didn't hear a thing."

"Jeff, I resent your implying that I'm somehow at fault. For all we know that shiny stuff you spent three hours slathering on the car yesterday might have caused some kind of problem. I clearly read on the tin that it should never be applied in direct sunlight which was exactly what you went and did. Even after I told you so."

"But why only on the mirrors?" he asked aloud, not addressing the question to her, which annoyed her even more.

"Hello, this is Jeff Sutherland? If you remember we bought the new Jeep Sahara from you guys about a week ago?"

Sitting across from him at the kitchen table Lisa hoped that he would remember that this was 'The Gentle Island'.

"What? Yes, I'm fine. Listen, there's some kind of problem with the side mirrors. The plastic is falling apart."

That, she thought, was an outright exaggeration.

"Yes. Well, sure. I *could* drive by tomorrow. Yeah, nine in the morning is good."

She heard the Jeep coming down the drive later in the afternoon and she could tell by the look on his face when he got out that things had gone well.

"They had no idea how it happened but they replaced both mirrors without making any fuss at all!" he said as he came through the kitchen door.

"*Brand-new* mirrors?"

"Brand-new mirrors."

The next morning she came back from checking the mailbox at the end of the drive and went straight upstairs.

VOICES

"Jeff, you'd better come outside." she said, standing in the doorway. Before he could say anything, she turned with a short, sharp spin and marched back down the hallway. He followed her down the stairs. Outside, the Jeep was parked in a scrap of shade under an arthritic old apple tree. He gave her a puzzled, slightly annoyed look.

"What?"

"Just *look*."

Then he saw it. Small, vicious looking holes in the black plastic top of one of the brand-new side mirrors.

"It's kids. It has to be some kind of vandalism."

"Vandalism? Jeff, our nearest neighbours are a mile away and they're a retired couple. And we would have heard something last night. After all, this is *Sturgeon*, not Parkdale."

"I just don't believe this can happen twice."

He stood by the sink staring out the window at the Jeep. It was parked as close to the house as possible, like a whale calf against the side of its giant mother. He leaned forward intently. She saw his back stiffen.

"No, it can't be." he whispered.

She joined him at the window but jerked back as a small black and gold shape shot past inches from the glass. It was a male chickadee, she realized, remembering an illustration from her copy of *Birds of Prince Edward Island*.

The chickadee was dive-bombing the Jeep. Once, twice and then a third time it flashed around both sides of the vehicle. As she watched, it landed on a side mirror and leaned its little body down from above to look into the mirror. As if it had received an electric shock it hopped back and began to peck furiously at the plastic surface. It paused, hopped to the edge and peered down into the mirror again. Once more, the little body quivered and the bird turned to peck the mirror in a blur of concentrated fury.

Jeff ran outside, clapping his hands, and the chickadee rocketed off into the trees. Lisa came out on the porch and Jeff turned to stare at her.

"I think I know what this is about," said Lisa. "Every time he flies by the Jeep he sees himself in the mirror and thinks it's another male. Another male on his territory. This other male is hiding inside the mirror and he wants to chase to him away."

"What do we do now?"

"Where were you?"

He was sprawled on the sofa, a beer bottle in one hand and two empties on the low table in front of him.

"Come and see."

Heaving himself up, he followed her out to the front porch. The Jeep was parked facing the house. Thick tubes of black, opaque fabric completely encased both of the side mirrors but with a foot or two of loose, slack material dangling from each one.

He was appalled. 'My God,' he thought, 'It looks like a pair of Snoopy ears.'

"Knee-length varicose vein socks," she pronounced, proudly, "and only $7.95 a pair at *Buy-Rite* in Montague."

VOICES

Technical Terms

"Thank you for calling Maritime Electric. It is Thursday, February the 6th at 10:45 am. We are currently aware of outages in the Rustico area and in Tracadie. Teams have been dispatched but restoration times are unknown at this time. If you would like to report an outage in a different area please stay on the line and one of our agents will be with you shortly."

This was their first winter on the Island since they had both retired and left Ottawa for good but they had been surprised by how savage the winter storms could be and how often the power was knocked out and how, when it was knocked out, it was knocked out for hours at a time.

"Thanks for calling Maritime Electric. How can I help you?"

A sweet, middle-aged female voice, he thought. Local accent and actually sounding truly concerned.

"Hello, we live in Gaspereaux and the lights have been flickering for about twenty minutes or so now."

"Oh, that's a let-down."

"It will be a *real* let-down if the power goes like it did yesterday for nine hours."

"Well dear, we had freezing rain and high winds yesterday." She sounded as if she was gently chiding him for being a bit obtuse or maybe even insensitive. "There were thousands of people who went without power yesterday."

"So I'm calling you to tell you that I think the power is about to go again."

"As I said, that's a let-down. Let-downs happen all the time."

Was she being sarcastic?

"What exactly do you mean when you say 'let-down'?"

"That's when the tree branches let down snow or melting ice on the lines and it causes the lights to flicker."

"That's a let-down?"

"Yes dear, and let-downs happen all the time. There's no point in worrying about them. Let-downs are hardly ever serious."

The Battle of Creed's Pond

It was late September and the skunks were at it again. Every morning Kristin woke up to see that more and more holes had been gouged out of her lawn. It looked like a helicopter gunship had machine-gunned her property, leaving only her house unscathed. They had even ripped out the stones around one end of the culvert at the foot of her drive to get at a wild bee's nest, leaving a sticky mess of honey combs stuck to the gravel.

"They're after grubs in the soil," said her nearest neighbour, Billy MacDonald, an easygoing, talkative fisherman in his forties. He had stopped in his car to chat with her while she was trying to repair the culvert.

"What can I do?" she asked.

"Well, the wife used to catch them in one of those humane traps you can get. They're so narrow that they can't raise their tails and spray, you see."

"Then what did she do?" Kristin asked. "Release them somewhere else?"

Billy laughed and looked at her with just a little bit of the wry pity he reserved for non-natives. "No, she picked up the trap by the handle and took it down to the road to Creed's pond there, and as she says, she'd 'baptize' them."

"But," he added, "that bastard from Toronto who has that big house down on the shore drove by one day and saw her doing it and he called the RCMP who sent over that young fellow from Wildlife, you know, one of the Gallant boys, and he gave her a warning."

"Thank God", thought Kristin.

"So," Billy continued, "I would get up at first light and go out with the rifle and hide behind the car and wait until they came onto the lawn. Got eight in two weeks but old Myrtle Condon across the road asked me to stop as it was waking her up too early."

"I remember," said Kristin, "when I first moved here last fall. I kept hearing bangs in the morning."

"Nobody's gonna be bothered now," said Billy, "except them damn skunks. I just drove into 'town this morning to buy *this*!"

He picked up a large menacing-looking metal object from the passenger seat. In Billy's big hairy, freckled hand it gleamed sleekly and bristled with anodized spars and rubberized turrets. It looked outlandish and utterly lethal.

"An Excalibur Matrix 750 with a recurved titanium bow," he informed her. "There's gonna be a whole lot less skunks in Kings County by the end of next month, I promise you that."

Three days later Kristin woke in the early morning with the reek of skunk spray filling the house. She slammed her bedroom window closed then hurried to the kitchen to close the windows that she had left open the night before. She cautiously stepped out onto the porch and was stunned by the intensity of the stink in the cool morning air.

She turned away but a motion on the road caught her eye. She stared in disbelief. A large skunk was coming down the middle of the country lane. It was walking erratically and something slim and silvery was sticking out on both sides of the animal's body. The skunk continued by her house, its gait stiff-legged and painful looking. She saw that one end of a shining metal bolt transfixing its body had a cruel-looking barbed head and the other end an incongruously bright fletching.

'My God, he's gone and shot one them,' she said to herself. Her eyes watering from the stink, she went back inside.

Half an hour later she dragged her garbage bin down the drive for pickup that day and was buffeted by the wake of a truck that roared by her. She recognized Billy's wife Winifred at the wheel. Winifred rarely drove the truck, preferring her old Malibu and even then never going above the speed limit.

Kristin felt a cold snake of alarm slide through her stomach. 'I'll fill the dishwasher," she thought, 'and then walk down to see if something's happened.'

She was at the end of her drive when the truck turned the corner in a flurry of gravel and raced down the road. Winifred slammed to a stop and lowered the window.

"Sorry, Hon, for driving so fast," she said, "but I had to go to Sobey's and it couldn't wait."

She looked flushed and agitated, not her normal placid self.

"Is something wrong?" asked Kristin.

"Hon," said Winifred, "you'd best stay put for the time being. I'll give you a call later."

She put the truck in gear and drove off. Kristin saw about a dozen large cardboard boxes on the flatbed.

The garbage truck came and went and Kristin walked down to the end of the drive to bring the bin back. It was then that she saw two vehicles appear at the head of the MacDonald's drive and slowly, carefully, turn onto the road.

She stood watching as this motorcade crept towards her. First came the truck with Winifred at the wheel and their teenage son, Tyler, in the passenger seat. Both had their heads swathed in what looked like old towels. The truck slid by her and Tyler mumbled out the window through his face covering, "Going to the pond."

As the truck crawled past she saw the flatbed was now filled with a jumble of ripped open cardboard packing cases and dozens of big tins of Heinz tomato juice rolling around, punctured and emptied.

She could see that the truck was slowly towing Winifred's old white Malibu but it was no longer white. The car was almost completely painted over with bright red tomato juice glistening in the morning light.

Then Kristin saw Billy. He came trudging along behind the crawling vehicles wearing nothing but a pair of skimpy briefs and flip flops. Like the Malibu, his big heavy body was drenched from head to toe in a glutinous sheet of coagulating red.

He passed by on his way to Creed's Pond, head down. He must have felt her standing there staring at him because he slowly raised his head and looked at her. His blue eyes shone with tears.

"The little bastard got me," he said softly.

VOICES

John Burck

Captain John A. Burck (Rtd) grew up in Amherstburg, a town on the Detroit River. Working for the local tug company during high school vacations made him decide on a career working on the water. After graduating, he signed a four-year apprenticeship with a deep-sea shipping company. He later enlisted in the RCMP taking the full land training before switching to the Marine Division. Leaving the Force he worked as Mate on a tug towing log rafts on the BC Coast. A job came open with BC Ferries where he had a chance to use his certificate as Mate of a Home Trade Steam Ship. That being a seasonal job and he himself about to be married, he wanted something more permanent.

He joined the Vancouver City Police Deptment where he worked on police boats, walked a beat in the Skid Row and worked a car in the West End, as well as being a member of the Mounted Squad for four years. Next came a job with the Port Moody Police. When he moved to PEI a position came open as Second Mate in the CNR Ferry Service. Laid off in the fall, he became an Instructor at the Summerside Marine School implementing a new three-week Marine Emergency Duties Program. After several Mate/Master jobs with marine towing companies he signed-on with Northumberland Ferries where he remained, as Mate/Master for twenty-seven years, until retirement.

He makes his home in Montague, PEI, spending half the year at his cottage overlooking the Northumberland Strait. Here he can enjoy watching the ferries and the waters that have been such a big part of his life.

FLASH
Planes Crash At S'side Base; Some Casualties

An undetermined number of Canadian Armed Servicemen were burned or injured in the spectacular crash of an Argus aircraft at CFB Summerside which occurred around 1:10 this afternoon. It could not be determined at press time if any were killed.

The Argus, which normally carries a crew of 16, was carrying out an emergency landing on three engines when the plane crashed into the tail section of an Electra aircraft which was parked at the time.

The Argus is reported to be completely destroyed and totally engulfed in flames as the Journal goes to press.

The source of the mechanical trouble in the Argus, a long-range patrol aircraft of the 415 VP Squadron, was not disclosed.

An observer near the crash site said that the Argus plane was burning and that the Base fire department was on the scene as well as ambulances and military police and RCMP.

The tail of the Electra was said to be completely severed. It is understood that there was no one in the Electra aircraft at the time of the crash.

The Electra is believed to be owned by Nordair and on loan to Environment Canada. The plane was stationed at the base and was being used to carry out routine ice patrols in the Gulf of St. Lawrence.

The Electra was described by one person knowledgeable in the airline industry as similar to the early civilian version of the Orion.

Further details of the crash could not be determined early this afternoon.

Prince County Hospital went on an immediate emergency basis with docotrs and off-duty nurses called in. Patients were being quickly discharged to make room for injured expected from the base.

Five injured were reported to have arrived by press time and several more were en route. Some crew members were believed to have escaped from the plane.

Base officials confirmed the crash and the fact that there were some injured. They said at the time of reporting they didn't know if there were any dead or not.

John Burck: The Crash of Argus Aircraft 737

The Crash of Argus Aircraft 737

An eyewitness account twenty-nine years later

    I was teaching a firefighting course as part of the Marine Emergency Duties program for adults at the Summerside Marine School the morning of March 31, 1977 and I had planned to go out to the fire grounds at CFB Summerside for some practical training that afternoon. So I sent the assistant instructor over to the nearby wharf to gather up some firewood. When he and his crew did not return I called the fire hall, looking for them. Sure enough, they were down at the fire grounds. I had planned to go after lunch but for some reason decided to go right away rather than leave those guys hanging around out there.

    When we arrived, the Base Fire Department's big foam trucks were rolling out. They told me an Argus Air Force plane was expected in soon on only three engines. This was no big deal as they often practiced such landings, but the trucks had to attend just in case. We were not to make smoke until she got in, but at the steel mock-up training structure the boys had already lit up. This wasn't an issue as it was confined to the building and we were going to train with breathing apparatus.

I was in the mock-up with my second student when the door flew open and a student said, "John, you better come and look at this!"

Pulling off my face mask I looked towards the hangars to see the Argus flying in completely engulfed in flames. Those big engines were screaming like some huge thing in agony.

For a moment I thought I was dreaming as the news over the past couple of days had been full of the collision of two jumbo jets on the runway on Tenerife and airplanes did not crash at the Summerside base!

She was heading in our general direction but then swung away slightly and sank out of sight. There was a loud bang, lots of smoke and an engine soared a few hundred feet up into the air.

Someone said, "What do we do?"

I didn't know. Did these planes carry weapons? Like the Mk 48 anti-sub torpedo?

"Lets go!" I said.

John Burck: The Crash of Argus Aircraft 737

I was about to run to the crash site when a student said, "Should we take extinguishers?"

This was madness. We were about to go to a blazing inferno and they wanted to take five pound extinguishers?

"Yeah, take 'em," I said, and we raced to the crash.

As we ran up a small rise between the crash site and the fire grounds we met a fellow in a flight suit carrying a flying helmet and a life vest.

"You OK?" I asked.

"Yeah, I'm alright," he replied and kept on walking away.

A group of survivors were huddled together on the grass in front of the nose of the aircraft. We found that some of them were hurt. One officer with a gash on his forehead seemed to be in command. I asked if he was OK and if there were any crew members still aboard.

"Never mind about me, look after my men," he said.

This struck me later as real leadership.

Just then I spotted someone trying to crawl away from the port side of the wreckage in an area just ahead of the wing. Flames were blowing down the wing from the fuselage but not quite at him. A student and I ran up and grabbed an arm each and hauled him away to the grass. There I faced him with my back to the plane and asked him if there were more crew members inside when suddenly a loud bang went off. Startled, the student and I grabbed his arms again and began to pull him even further away but much faster this time. While doing this, for whatever reason, I said, "We're going to move you, OK?"

"I'd be very grateful if you would," he replied, casually.

Again, later, I thought, 'How brave to be so cool,' looking at the blazing plane with stuff exploding inside and him with a broken femur.

While I was occupied with this crew member two other of my students were hauling a second survivor away from the same spot. This was Captain Bridgen, who had broken his hip and who had been sitting with another officer in a compartment handy to the port wing.

When the aircraft hit the ground the deck beneath their feet buckled so severely that their legs were seriously injured. I heard

VOICES

later that a port-side propeller had torn off and ripped a hole in the skin of the plane right where they were sitting. Unaware that they had been badly hurt, they both jumped out onto the wing only to have their legs give out on them. This was why they needed help getting clear of the scene.

Captain Bridgen, as I learned later, hailed from a small town in Ontario close to where I was raised and his first cousins, some of them my age, had lived only a block away from me.

All the students in my class were still in proper firemen's bunker or turn-out gear, and I still had the Scott air pack bottle strapped on my back. It was overcast, I remember, and windy. The ground was soft and muddy.

Suddenly, one of the students called out to me from the area of the starboard wing, "John, come quickly, there's a man on fire here!"

I began to run towards him but it was like being in a dream. My bottle and gear seemed so heavy. I was tired and I was slipping on the mud. Above all, I did not want to see this.

I found an airman lying on his back amidst the wreckage from the wing. I had picked up a five pound dry chemical fire extinguisher that someone had brought and quickly discharged some of it onto him. The flames went out and I swept away any other flames burning near. I turned away to move on, but saw that he was on fire again. He had somehow been drenched with fuel as he escaped from the aircraft down the starboard wing. He was Sergeant Arsenault, the flight engineer.

I immediately sprayed him again and swept back the flames again. Same result, only now the extinguisher was empty. I pulled him off the wreckage and beat out the flames with my gloved hands. The fire under the torn metal of the wing had escaped the extinguishers spray of powder, so as soon as I had moved the stream away the flames had re-ignited his fuel-soaked clothing. He was in extremely bad shape.

While this was happening, someone nearby called out, "There's another one here!"

It was Major Hawkes, face down and on fire, struggling to get up.

"We have an extinguisher, but its foam. Should we use it?" the student asked me.

"Yes! "I roared at him. "Use anything. Right now!"

An old-style army ambulance rolled up so we readied the injured for evacuation. Trouble was encountered getting the rear door open but finally it did. On loading the injured it was found that one of the students had used a tourniquet on a severely bleeding leg wound with exposed bone which in this case was the right thing to do. Some of my class had covered the injured with their bunker coats. The coats went off with the injured to the hospital but we did get them back.

A fire truck pulled up and I expected someone to say, "OK boys, we'll take over now." Instead, an NCO firefighter said, "Glad you are here," and went off to attack the fire.

So we carried on.

At this time a yellow street-flusher water truck pulled up as well. The driver did not get out, having only been told to go to the scene. I knew this guy could pump water, having used him on the fire grounds the year before as there had been no hydrant there then.

A foam truck that had blown a full load onto the fire cast off a hand line (hose) and the driver had raced back to the fire hall to reload. The hose was there. The water truck was there. So I decided to use them.

We tried hooking the hose onto a valve on the truck but we found the handle on the valve stem was missing. So we took it off to put it on the other outlet only to find the pipe cap on the outlet was seized shut. A fire truck had arrived by now so we got a pipe wrench from its tool chest to remove the cap and we hooked up successfully.

We now put the hose to work on the fire. A second line was run from the hydrant on the fire grounds. This too was brought to bear on the blaze.

I had noticed when the first firemen arrived that the Deputy Chief and a Private, followed by one of our students, had entered the rear of the plane in search of casualties. None were found. The front part of the plane was well engulfed in flames so it must have been one scary place.

While manning our hose on the downwind side we got a fright when a heavy gust of wind ripped a large section about ten feet square of aluminum plating off the tail above our heads and sent it sailing down the runway. Luckily, no one was in its way.

Another foam truck appeared and shot another load into the flames. Some of the stream went over the top of the wreckage, covering our two men at the hose from head to toe with foam. No one laughed at them. Not this time.

I had noticed one of the planes seats sitting upright on the tarmac next to the fuselage. I couldn't figure out how it could have gotten there as they were bolted to the flight deck. Afterwards, I learned that there had been a crewman seated in it, strapped in. When the Argus had clipped another aircraft in mid-flight and then burst into flame this crewman had told himself to close his eyes and hold his breath so as not to inhale any gases. After the impact of the crash landing he had opened his eyes to find himself still sitting in his seat but on the tarmac of the runway. He didn't stick around to find out how he had gotten there. Instead, he unbuckled and tore off down the runway as fast as he could go.

A truck was sent out to bring him and another runner back in.

The fire was now pretty well under control, so we backed away.

Then my assistant pulled out his pack of cigarettes and prepared to light up. The Deputy Chief scowled at him. "I'd just as soon you didn't do that," he grimly advised.

Point taken. The ground was soaked in aviation fuel.

With thanks from the professionals, we gathered up whatever of our gear we could find, loaded up and went back to the school. I was surprised when we got there to see how early in the day it actually was.

So much had happened in so short a time.

Soon, we were visited by the military who requested that we write out everything we had done or had seen. This we did and before leaving they warned us not to speak to the press or to give out statements as an official investigation was underway. So, very few people knew about the role this Marine School fire-fighting class had played in the rescue. I kept expecting to hear details about the crash in the news but I never did.

However, a year later the whole class was invited to the Base for the dedication of a memorial plaque in the chapel. When we arrived on the day we found two large flights of airmen waiting for us there in an enormous hangar. I figured it was an awards ceremony about to take place or perhaps we were there to witness the issuing of promotions. But I was truly surprised when we were called to come forward and accept Certificates of Merit from this, the 415 Squadron, as well as Certificates of Merit from the Royal Canadian Humane Society presented by none other than the Chief Justice of Prince Edward Island.

Parade was then dismissed.

It had all been for us!

We were then invited to the officers mess for drinks and lunch.

A few days later at Government House the Lieutenant Governor presented each of us with the Red Cross CJRW Lifesaving Award.

Being recognized for doing something worthwhile was all very nice. Especially for a couple of the boys who were only known for heavy drinking back in their little hometowns.

They had come through when it had mattered most.

I had always attempted to make my Lifeboat and Survival First Aid and Firefighting Training as realistic as I possibly could, but this incident had gone way beyond any classroom realism I had ever achieved.

Nevertheless, that class of students had responded without hesitation and with courage and had done a commendable job.

I was proud of them then.

And I still am, now.

VOICES

A Believable FERRY Tale

Everyone wants to be the Captain.

Of course, on a fine summer day with the sun shining down on a lovely flat sea, who wouldnt?

Then as your ferry approaches land you see this guy in a fancy uniform with four gold rings on his cuffs, peaked cap with gold braid on the visor and looking pretty sharp. He saunters up the deck and disappears into the wheelhouse.

Interested, you peer through a gap in the curtains and see him talking to two men.

The one with the epaulettes is obviously a Mate and the other fellow is steering which would make him the Quartermaster. Nearing the berth, the guy with the most stripes takes over and neatly slips the ship alongside and up to the ramp so the ships traffic can be unloaded. There is a jangle of bells as he swings the handles of the Engine Room telegraph to *Finished with Engines* and with that, he exits the bridge and proceeds into the cafeteria and chats with staff.

Soft job, wouldn't you say? But what about the not so nice days?

My first time up on the Northumberland Ferries Line ship, *Prince Nova*, as Master was a memorable one. The shift started with a powerful sou'easter. This was a bad wind in direction and strength as it was very hard to keep the stern up to make her fast under the Wood Islands ramp. It was frustrating work knowing the passengers were wondering why NFL didnt get someone who could drive this thing. Eventually, I did learn how to 'drive' her and actually enjoyed doing so.

If it was bad at the dock then conditions on the Strait were no picnic. It was necessary to alter quite a few degrees off course to

John Burch: A Believable FERRY Tale

ease the effects of the rough seas. Heavy pitching and rolling were hard on the ship, not to mention the passengers. Many would be seasick and some even be wondering why we had taken them out there under those conditions. The Captain surely must be mad.

The worst experience I encountered that year was the dreaded FOG!

It was a lovely, calm, sunny day. Occasional fog patches had been encountered on the way across from Caribou. As we approached Wood Islands (where, it was rumoured they made the fog) we met a dense blanket of fog. How we cursed and hated that stuff.

The old radar left a lot to be desired. Distant targets were generally pretty good. Inside work, such as entering harbour, was made difficult due to the large amount of clutter obscuring the breakwaters where we had to go between them to get in.

The tidal prediction was for a falling tide so we set up to the west so that the set would push us down to the harbour mouth. The bridge watch plus the fo'c'sle head party all strained their eyes looking for the first sight of land, especially of the breakwaters or as we called them, the 'steels'.

"Theres one of them!"
"Where?"
"On the starboard beam."
"Oh, s***!"

They were not supposed to be there. *Full Astern* was applied, everything she had, as she glided smoothly towards the sandy beach beside the west steel.

Since speed had been reduced earlier it did not take much to stop her. We didn't go aground but we were close to it. As we backed off the visibility became zero again, which totally confused us.

A call from the fo'c'sle head was accompanied by the seaman pointing to something off our starboard side. It was the buoy, the red one stationed off the harbor mouth. We knew where we were now. We knew something else from the water tail on the buoy - the tide was rising instead of falling as predicted. That was what had put us in such a bad position. You could never trust the tide off that port.

That experience really shook me up.

I could see lawsuits, the loss of my certificate and lots more if my actions caused any passenger injury. However the next year my confidence was restored when the first fogs were not thick and everything worked out right.

Funny thing though. Later, after these two terrifying incidents, whenever the ship was rearing and plunging in heavy seas or blinded by fog, I could not find anyone interested in changing jobs with me.

Nobody wanted to be Captain.

John Burck: The Stuff of Legends

The Stuff of Legends

Yes, this guy definitely was the stuff legends were made of.

Captain Henry B. 'Harry' Squarey was one of CNR Ferries' Masters on the Borden/Cape Tormentine run. He was on the *Holiday Island* when I joined her as Second Mate back in the 70's.

The majority of the crew was openly friendly but this guy was sullen and scowling and he obviously did not like me. Nor did I like him. If there were more like him around I wouldn't last long here.

Laid-off in the fall, I was called back in the spring and was assigned to pick up the *Lucy Maud Montgomery* in North Sydney as she was heading for dry dock in Montreal.

On the bus I was excited at the prospect of a 'sea' voyage with a great port like Montreal at the end of it.

"Who's the Skipper?" I asked my seatmate and fellow Second Officer, Louie Ward.

"Harry," he replied.

'Oh no!' I thought. This obviously was going to be hell for me. I told Louie my troubles and his reply was that Harry was a good guy. He just didn't know me. He was like that with all strangers. "You'll like him," he insisted.

"Yeah. Right."

We picked up the ship without incident and set sail up the St. Lawrence for Montreal. Although I had been ashore for a number of years, I felt confident, having been Third Mate on a deep sea freighter during my apprenticeship. Every now and then Harry, the 'Old Man', would stalk out onto the bridge.

"Whe're we now?" he'd grunt and I would point to the course line on the chart.

"Here," I would say, "A little more west from our last fix."

The deep-sea boys used to refer to this part of the river as Spiritual Navigation. The navigator would take bearings of the prominent churches and put them on the chart to fix our position.

Soon Harry would start staying a little longer and eventually he began to tell stories. I knew then that I had been accepted. Soon Louie wandered in, although he would not take over the watch for a couple of hours. We enjoyed Harry's stories and he liked telling them.

He told us about working with his father on a schooner as a lad. They hauled freight along the Newfoundland coast, where they lived. No living quarters were provided, so he and the hired man had to sleep among the cargo. He described his shipmate as a dirty old bugger. He was about to find out just how dirty.

One morning he was with his father on deck when his old man asked him if he had messed himself. He was taken aback by such a question from his father and denied having done such a thing. But his father was sniffing around him for the source of the stench.

"It's dem boots!" his father said.

"Can't be!" Harry protested. "Dese boots is on for the first time." To prove his point he began pulling his boots off. An intense stink filled the air.

What Harry didn't know was that while he was asleep in the hold with the hired hand, the hand had needed to relieve himself. Finding a suitable container would save him a trip up and out on deck to the ship's rail and Harry's tall rubber boots were handy. When Harry figured this out and confronted him, he vehemently denied the accusation. He was big and ugly enough to know Harry was no threat to him.

It seemed that everything happened to Harry. So it was not totally unexpected that while we were having breakfast one morning something would happen. While Harry was buttering a piece of his

John Burck: The Stuff of Legends

toast a chunk of warm butter flew off the toast and landed smack in the middle of his tie. It was Fate underlining the fact that everything *did* happen to Harry. When we saw the expression on his face we all instantly decided not to laugh or at least not while he was around.

We returned from refit to find that Harry and I would be shipmates on the *Lucy* for the summer schedule. There were six boats running from Borden that summer. All the berths were taken so we had to go up the coast to Summerside to tie up each night. We were the extra ship that only was used when traffic was heavy. When the others handled traffic we would be sent off to tie up.

As coincidence would have it we had a friend in common in Ontario. Harry had been sent to Windsor, Ontario to take command of a railway barge being pushed across the river to Detroit, Michigan and back. The local tug hired was the *Atomic* and her skipper was a best friend and shipmate of mine, Captain Cliff Morrison. The *Atomic* was a boat from my nearby hometown and was the first ship I ever worked on. Its a small world.

We got off to a rocky start but after sailing with him for a few months I found Captain Harry Squarey to be a good shipmate, a fine seaman and a good friend.

VOICES

Gary Gray

Gary's family came to Prince Edward Island from Scotland by way of Nova Scotia. He was born and raised near Coleman, PEI. In 2002 Gary suffered a massive stroke and has battled his way to what he now warmly refers to as his *new normal*. He has adjusted his life in order to recover many of the abilities he has lost. He is working hard to help others affected by stroke find *their* new normal.

Gary has written articles about his own stroke experience as well as a four-page information piece about the need for an Acute Stroke Recovery Unit for Prince Edward Island. He joined the Montague Library Writers Guild in 2008 in order to stimulate his brain into recovery from the effects of his stroke. As a member, he has been inspired to write personal and family memoirs of his early years as a native Islander. He also continues to publish articles - mostly on the Internet - related to stroke, technology and art. Find more information about Gary online at: *http://en.gravatar.com/garydotgray*

When he isn't writing, Gary enjoys taking in the Island's beauty on his daily walks and meeting friends for tea. Most of all he is happy to once again be able to enjoy the relaxed lifestyle Prince Edward Island is famous for.

VOICES

Yellow School

Have you ever had the opportunity to attend a one-room school? Compared to the schools of today it's hard to imagine twenty or thirty kids age six to fourteen of eight different grades all in one classroom with one teacher. Today there are separate teachers for every subject and a separate classroom as well.

Come with me, to a place where 'the three R's' were taught, as they were known. Reading, 'Riting and 'Rithmetic.

Reading was usually done from a Dick and Jane type book for the lower grades and a more formal reader for the higher ones. It included oral spelling exercises which were more like competitions. Writing was centred around what was known as The MacLean's Method of writing and included creating written pieces like 'What Did I Do On My Summer Vacation'. Arithmetic involved the basics of addition, subtraction, division and multiplication or 'times'. Oral exercises were common with questions such as two times two or two times four. As a student ascended through the grade structure, other subjects were added like Health, Geography and History.

On one side of the large single classroom were high, west-facing windows. Desks were arranged in rows across the classroom smallest to largest from left to right. A double wide blackboard dominated the front of the classroom featuring examples of the MacLean's Method of writing above and a chalktray with pieces of chalk and erasers below.

The teacher's desk and chair sat at the front facing the rows of student desks. On the desk sat the bell used to announce the end of recess and dinner hour. Within a drawer of the desk lived the leather strap that appeared when misbehaviour warranted discipline.

Large maps of the country and the region hung on the available wall space as well as a large framed picture of the current reigning British monarch. The British flag known as the Union Jack hung near the front of the classroom.

Along the east and south sides of the classroom there were five separate rooms. Two of the east side rooms were cloakrooms, a boys' and a girls'. In these rooms were large, high, east-facing windows, a long coat rack with hooks on the west wall and a chemical toilet in one corner surrounded by a closed cubicle for privacy. Centred between the cloakrooms was an entry room used to store wood for the stove in winter to heat the building. These rooms also acted as buffer spaces to protect the classroom from cold Island east winds.

The two separate rooms on the south of the building consisted of a pump room and a library. Both rooms had large, high south-facing windows. The pump room had a low cupboard with a white enameled sink on top. A drain ran out through the south wall and emptied into the schoolyard. Other storage space resided behind several small doors in the lower part of the cupboard. The only water that found its way into the pump room was that carried in using an old metal bucket from the outside pump next to the woodshed just west of the schoolhouse.

The library housed a couple of older style bench-type desks, which were located on the west side of the room. On the east wall

Carleton Lot 6 No. 9 One Room School circa 1956

was a large, high, book cupboard containing a sparse hodgepodge of outdated books. No one ever used the library to read in. It was used mainly on dreary, cold, wet days simply as a place to hang out.

Outside, was the area of space most often used during recess and dinner hours. The school property was about an acre in size. The perimeter of the property was marked with a green wood and wire fence including an iron and wire gate allowing entry from the roadway that ran along the east side of the school property

To the north of the school was a well-worn area where Ball was played. Other games included Hide 'n' Seek, Red Rover, Lepo, and Simon Says. Of all the games, Ball was the favourite. It allowed for the greatest number of participants to enjoy an activity together involving teams.

Other landmarks on the property included the flag pole to the south of the school and the woodshed and outdoor pump to the west. The coasting hill was located just off school property to the southwest. A little further to the west beyond a wooded area was the brook.

The school itself was a single wooden structure about thirty-six by forty-eight feet in size. Wooden shingles covered the exterior. The walls were painted yellow and the roof was oiled black. Trim was painted white and a small gable roofed porch protruded from the east side to allow entry. A single one-and-a-half by eight-foot sign painted black was mounted above the exterior of the porch announcing to all the name of the school, *Carleton Lot 6 No 9*.

The one room school is another unique piece of the history of Prince Edward Island. I appreciate the fact that I was able to be a part of it.

Thank you for coming along to return to a place of fond memories and good times. I will never forget the days of the one room school and the lessons as well as the friendships gained there.

Gary Gray: Gray's Transport

Gray's Transport

Today is not a quiet day. It's a 'storm day', as they call it here on the Island. A day when the winds whip in from the northeast bringing snow with them. Lots of snow. It's the kind that whites out the landscape and piles itself into four foot drifts, making it impossible to travel even the shortest distance.

This is a day to stay at home, out of the storm. A day to read a book or sort through pictures that inspire memories of the past. As I enjoy the warmth of a mug of tea while relaxing on my recliner with a soft blue throw over my legs, my eyes are drawn to just one picture. It's a black and white photograph taken sometime in the late

Left to Right the GRAY boys: Earl, Cecil, David (my dad), Everett, Stewart and Wilbur

1940's.

A transport truck fills almost the entire photograph. Along the top of the box is a light twelve-inch band of what I remember from other pictures was bright yellow. On this yellow band in what I recall as green uppercase letters are the words *GRAY'S TRANSPORT O'LEARY P. E. Island*. On the side of the transport truck box was a large yellow circle with the word *GRAY'S* painted on it, also in green, both horizontally and vertically in the same way that the word *BAYER* appears on a Bayer's aspirin tablet.

In front of this truck, standing shoulder to shoulder are six well-dressed men ranging in age from their late twenties to late thirties.

One of these six men is my father. The other five are uncles. All six have now lived and died. I begin thinking of what it must have been like for them then? How did they come to be together for this picture? What events in life had brought them there?

To answer these questions we need to travel back to an even earlier time. A time when the economy on Prince Edward Island was not so strong. A time when young people went off to what was known as the Boston States, as Islanders called the Boston area, to find work.

Two such people were a girl named Rose Dennis from Port Hill and a boy named William Gray from The Dock near Alberton.

William found work as a carpenter working on building sites in Waltham and Rose found work at the Waltham Watch Factory where she met Eva and Hannah, two sisters of William's who were also working there.

William and Rose met, courted, married and had a family of two children while living in the Boston area.

Their first child was born at Port Hill on Prince Edward Island, as Rose had returned to the Island to be with her mother for the delivery. Their second child was born in Waltham.

Meanwhile, back on Prince Edward Island, William's mother Sarah had died. His father was now alone and was in need of support with the farm. As was the custom on the Island at that time the young couple moved their family back to Alberton to care for William's ageing father. It was their plan that this arrangement would be for a limited time and that they would return to the States at some point in the future.

As it turned out, only their first two children returned to Boston. William and Rose would have seven more children and continue to live on the Island. After William's father died William also died at a relatively young age leaving Rose and the children to manage the farm. As the children grew up during the 20's and 30's the farm became the main means of living for the Gray family. In the early 30's my dad met a girl from Cascumpec at a local church meeting community event. By 1938 they had courted, married and began their family with the arrival of two children.

Life was not easy for my parents or my father's siblings who were also starting families at this time. The stock market crash of 1929 and the Great Depression of the 30's challenged the economy of the Island as well as most of the North American continent. The farms of Prince Edward Island provided a small measure of stability through the food that could be produced on them.

World events were soon to unleash a second world war that would last from 1939 to 1945. Canada had been a part of the Allied Forces during the First World War and would be again. Young men and women from all across Canada would sign up to serve their country and that would include Prince Edward Island.

From my father's family of seven children in Canada six would volunteer for active duty. Only one was left to do the important work of tending the farm while the others all served as part of Canada's contribution of personnel to the war effort. Four boys and two girls.

The two who had returned to the States had not enlisted, and as well, one brother on the Island remained on the farm.

When the boys returned from the war, they came back to their families on Prince Edward Island. The girls got married, one to an airman and the other to a sailor and both couples went to live in Ontario.

With the training they had received while in the military and by pooling any savings and discharge pay, my father and two of his brothers decided to start a freight transport business with the purchase of three trucks. They also needed a location to warehouse freight as well as to maintain and repair the trucks. My father bought a small parcel of land on the Western Road in Carleton Lot 6. He established a warehouse/garage on it large enough to meet the task.

With three trucks, a warehouse/repair shop, two drivers and a driver/mechanic, *GRAY'S TRANSPORT* had begun.

Still holding the picture, my mind focuses even more clearly on how this was a reflection of many Island families during the first half of the 1900's. Many young people went to the Boston States for work. Families were self-reliant and supported parents as the need was required. The farm became a valuable resource to sustain families during the Depression of the 30's and the war years of the 40's. Many Island families had sons and daughters volunteer to serve overseas during the Second World War. Self-employment became a more common means to gain a secure income after the war was over.

I think about growing up on the Island as part of the baby boom that began in the late 40's and my heart grows warm with appreciation for a family who endured hard and dangerous times to provide for me the carefree childhood days during the 50's and 60's.

[Additional family information shown below has been taken with thanks to the *Wartime Recognition Bookle; Volume 6* published by the Prince Edward Island Royal Canadian Legion Command. These are the members of my dad's family who served during the Second World War:

"David was born in Alberton, PEI, on September 23, 1914. He joined the Army and trained with Engineers in Alberta and was sent overseas where he helped build Bailey Bridges in Holland when Canadians liberated Holland. David passed away on April 10, 1987.

"Everett was born in Alberton, PEI, on May 30, 1916. He served with the Royal Canadian Artillery and Ordinance Corps overseas. He joined immediately after Canada declared war and served until the war was over.

"Helen was born in Alberton, PEI, on November 27, 1922. She joined the Canadian Womens Army Corps and trained in Kitchener, ON, before going overseas as a switchboard operator in London, England. War ended, but because telephones were needed for administration, Helen did not return until the end of January 1946.

"Ruth was born in Alberton, PEI, on July 12, 1924. She joined the Canadian Womens Army Corps with her sister, Helen, and trained in Kitchener, ON. She served in Halifax, NS, until her discharge. Ruth was the only one of the six children that did not go overseas.

"Stewart was born in Alberton, PEI, on May 30, 1916. He joined the Royal Canadian Artillery with his twin brother, Everett. They trained together and both went overseas. Stewart passed away on May 17, 1977.

"Wilbur was born in Alberton, PEI, on December 21, 1920. He served in the Service Corps driving large trucks overseas. He became ill in England and was sent home on hospital ship Lady Nelson. He was operated on at Camp Hill Hospital in Nova Scotia. When he was discharged, he had had a kidney removed. Wilbur passed away on January 28, 1991."]

Blue Bicycle

When I was nine years old my older brother gave me a bicycle. Not just an ordinary bicycle, but one that he rebuilt from a discarded CCM frame he had found one day. He started with the old frame including a good, bare pedal mechanism and handlebars.

He bought the various bits and pieces needed to rebuild the bike. Front and rear hubs for the wheels, spokes, rims, tires, and tubes. As he assembled the pieces the wheels emerged, ready to be connected to the newly painted deep blue frame. New fenders to match the frame, a drive chain, chain guard and pedals were added. Then came a brand new brown adjustable seat and blue handgrips for the chrome handlebars. Multi-coloured streamers were added to

Gary with Blue Bicycle age 9

the handgrips and a shiny battery powered horn with a black activation button to the handlebars.

To a kid today, it might have been a plain old bicycle from a style long since replaced by much fancier multi-speed racing, mountain and trickster bikes. But in those earlier days, and to me in particular, it was the best bike in the world.

As I grow older and full of the deep appreciation for the love of family I feel my heart expand in my chest with the remembered warmth of my brother's love. This was only one of the many gifts that my brother shared with me during his short lifetime.

Terry Kerr

Terry Kerr came to live on Prince Edward Island in 1995 and over the years she has pursued her interests in crafts and writing as the Island landscapes and marine life have inspired her.

She lives on the shore in a log home and has been involved in organizations that promote stewardship of our environment, learning Island crafts and helping out in the community.

Born in Toronto and raised in Manitoba, Terry finds many similarities between the Prairie peoples and Islanders. Their caring nature, willingness to help anyone in trouble and the joy of life are alike between these two provinces. She feels very much at home on PEI.

Terry began writing years ago as a hobby and she has written a play, several poems and stories and is planning to publish her first children's book this year.

VOICES

Celebrate Winter!

We are Canadians...we are Islanders...we celebrate Winter!

We spend the season ensuring that the crafts of our ancestors are not forgotten; learning and teaching rug braiding, step dancing, rug hooking, quilting, fiddle playing, clogging. We write, tell stories, paint and carve.

We are in the woods cutting trees for firewood, mending our lobster traps for the coming season, snowshoeing, tobogganing, listening for owls, watching for eagles and hawks, following the tracks of the fox and coyote, skiing.

Our homes are lively as we embrace the season. We have potluck suppers with our friends and families, community fundraisers for Islanders in need, church suppers, impromptu ceilidhs when we sing Islander Allan Rankin's song, "Raise the Dead of Winter". Some of us even bring in the New Year by plunging into the icy local rivers. We love the fiddles, guitars, pianos, stomping feet, clapping hands, shouts of joy!

We can be silent too, as we reflect on our good fortune, sad times, friends and family who are away, relatives and companions who have gone on before us leaving us with our memories - the beauty of a snowfall, the wind, the sunrise and the setting sun - our blessings.

We are Islanders - either born here or by choice. Wherever we have come from we celebrate life here in all its glory, embracing our winter and waiting for spring.

The Ocean

The Island sky stretched vast and blue, fields meeting the horizon.
I thought no other place could steal my heart,
But then I saw the Ocean.

Island lupines, sweet smelling earth, songs of the piping plover,
Spring had come and my heart swelled, gazing at the splendour.
I thought no other place could bring such joy,
But then I heard the Ocean.

The power of the Island storm flattening the grasses,
Clouds black, ominous, thundering, screeching winds
Nothing could equal the terror of the hurricane force,
Except, the angry Ocean.

The bleakness of the Island winter, icy sheets of frost,
My son, he has not known that cold, that desperate ache for warmth.
Nor does he love, as I do now, Prince Edward Island.

And yet he knows the pounding waves, the surging tides, the squalls.
The Ocean calls and he will go and seek his own fulfillment.
And he, like I, will gaze in awe and love the mystic Ocean.

VOICES

The Deadly Storm

The storm was born in the great northern forests from the union of snow and wind. As it flew out of its birthplace, it began to grow and feel its burgeoning power. By the time it reached the Island, the storm had become sinister, revelling in its evil intent. As the wind grew it tested its voice, screeching and howling, the snow partner now as hard and deadly as jagged shards of glass. And still it came, its giant eye searching for victims, those unfortunate souls, man and beast, that stood in its path.

He was coming home after a long week of travel, selling automotive parts to the country garages that were spread across the Maritimes. It had been a hard week and he was tired. Sales had been poor and the hotels with their seedy bars had seemed worn and cold. His radio was broken and it wasn't until he was on the ferry heading for the Island that he had learned about the incoming storm. He hadn't foreseen the speed with which the storm was approaching and as he drove off the ferry his thoughts were on his family. Imagining his wife and children deep in preparation for the traditional Friday homecoming meal, he smiled as he anticipated the animated stories of their week with all its ups and downs of Island life. With his thoughts on his family and face towards home, he didn't notice the blackening sky behind him. He didn't see the eye casting around, then lighting with evil glee on his small speeding car.

She had been listening to the radio all day and was clearly worried as the news of the monster storm had others scrambling for safety. She had gathered her children around and made all of the preparations that needed to be made. The rabbit was in the garage safe within his cage. The chicken coop was locked, their prize poultry bedded down and secure and the dogs were in the basement, pacing and whining as they sensed the dropping pressure of the atmosphere.

The storm roared towards him, racing across the barren fields of harvested wheat and potatoes, gathering the killing speed and destructive power that would place it in the history books as one of the deadliest winter storms in history.

Too late he looked behind him, saw the monster and was swallowed into the abyss. The road disappeared as the wind and snow thundered all around him sending the little car careening across the road. He fought to gain control and with adrenalin induced strength kept the car upright, hugging the side of the road using the gravel as an aid for the wheels. He slowed his passage knowing that the car and this road were his only lifelines.

She stood at the window looking into the howling vast whiteness beyond and prayed for his safety. Perhaps, she thought, he had taken shelter at a farm or in an abandoned barn. Surely he had heard of the storm's approach and soon would be calling, telling her that he was safe and would be home later. However, as time went on her dread grew and she instinctively knew that he was out there alone and in terrible danger. The children gathered around her looking into her face for reassurance. What they saw filled them with unease as they saw the worry in her eyes. As she looked down at their small sweet faces she rallied and, scarce heard above the screaming banshee wails of the wind, she began to comfort them by telling them stories of heroes and their Dad.

It took no notice of the helplessness of animals or humans as it swept the landscape clear of life. Nothing could stand in its way as it struck down and froze everything in its path. The monster storm had not lost any of its strength and it continued on its journey into the history books, sweeping through towns, slamming the great oak, birch and spruce trees into the ground and toppling any building that stood in its way.

He had to abandon his car. He could go no further as the snowdrifts rose up in front of him and blocked his passage. He tied his woolen scarf around his hat, buttoned up his coat, put on his gloves and stepped out into the howling gale. His breath was sucked away by the wind, his face instantly a myriad of cuts from the needle shards of the icy snow as he put one foot in front of the other. He was almost home and his only hope was to follow the edge of the road feeling his way. But the cold was piercing his body and he could barely see.

She stood at the window watching until she could bear it no longer. She turned into the kitchen the need to keep her hands busy overwhelming her. Dusk was falling and the candles were lit making the kitchen into a soft retreat from the panic that threatened to engulf her.

"Mama! I saw him!" her little girl screamed. "I saw Daddy. But he walked past our house!"

She flew into the living room and strained to see into the gloom"

"It was him," her daughter cried, "I saw his grey coat. Where is he going?"

Now the sobs of despair shook her body as she realized that he had come so close to safety and had failed to see his haven.

Then suddenly he was there, falling into her arms as he burst through the door. Laughing and sobbing he shook his fist at the demon outside as it screamed overhead in frustrated fury.

Island Healing

Coming home, towards the river, clouds blackening the sky
I pondered where the geese had gone and breathed a gentle sigh.
Then suddenly a ray of light, the sun was breaking through
And bursting forth like laughing children, sunbeams fairly flew.

They quickly leapt across the land, surrounding every tree
And covered fields in brightest amber, happy to be free.
The dead grass shone with lights of gold, the maples vibrant red
And all my world began anew, my soul, once more was fed.

Those Island sunbeams touched my heart, and so enlarged my day
That all my thoughts turned to my son, my son so far away.
He sees the beauty of this place, he sees beyond the pain
To where we all should go to love, to be renewed again.

When he comes home I'll hold him tight and feel his beating heart
And watch his son and daughter laugh as through the woods they dart.
He'll show them how to laugh and live and teach that all belong
To have the courage and the faith to sing their Island song.

VOICES

Sheila Mallory

Born in Toronto, Ontario, Sheila Mallory attended schools there and taught in Toronto and other cities in Ontario. Some years later Sheila studied theology and was ordained by the United Church of Canada. On her first appointment she was sent to the Nashwaak Charge in New Brunswick. In the small village of Taymouth on the Nashwaak River she met her husband Guy. Guy owned a woodland property and the couple lived there happily in a log home. Although it was a challenge Sheila adapted to the radical change from Toronto to Taymouth.

After nine years on that Charge the time came to move on. Sheila wanted to return to Ontario, or serve the Church in Western provinces. That did not happen. During the last few years a lady from Victoria, Prince Edward Island had persistently phoned to see if Sheila was considering a move to another Charge. Those invitations were declined. When it was known that Sheila would be moving, she tried again. This time Sheila felt that she owed her caller at least a visit. In November of 1990 Sheila and Guy took the ferry to meet with Jean Howatt of Victoria.

When Sheila saw the shores of Prince Edward Island and journeyed through Borden to Tryon and Crapaud she was captivated. She wanted very much to find work on the Island. As it happened she became the first woman to serve the Tryon-Hampton Charge.

Previously Sheila had heard about the Murray Harbour-Murray River Charge in Kings County. A colleague had been sent there and reports were favourable.

When an opportunity opened to serve there she took it.

This move turned out to be a wise decision. Both Sheila and her husband loved the community, feeling accepted and included. Officially, Sheila retired in 1998 returning with her husband to New Brunswick. After finding a home on the Island, Sheila found it hard to re-adapt. After some unsettling years the couple parted. Eventually, Sheila returned to the Island to live in Montague, continuing to serve King's County United Churches.

At present Sheila involves herself in community activities — Seniors College, Atlantic Fitness programs as well as church life. She enjoys her home and garden, Lily her cat and especially her friends.

Sheila learned the discipline and pleasure of writing after studying literature in University, writing reports during teaching years, and preparing sermons over a period of thirty years. She came to appreciate more and love the world of nature after her church placements in Atlantic Canada.

The Sparrow

It's an ill wind that blows no one any good (Old Mariners' Proverb). Prince Edward Island is well known for its wind, which is not always gentle.

On a windy day my husband Guy, my niece Christina and I drove to downtown Charlottetown to rent a bicycle for her. We stopped on University Avenue outside a sports shop and noticed a clump of debris, mostly dried grass that had been blown against the building by the wind. It was the remnant of a bird's nest, carried by the wind from a nearby tree or high wire complex. We found a baby bird barely protected by the strewn nest. Mother was not near; only one newly hatched, naked baby with no feathers. We agreed to try and rescue it. Christina found a good-sized box in the shop. Guy gently put the bird in the box along with strands of its nest, carefully closing the top.

After arriving at our home in Crapaud our main problem became how to keep the bird alive. I found an eyedropper, filled it with water and tried to drop the water into its mouth. The bird kept opening and closing its beak making it difficult to give it a drop or two. I got the idea of stroking its chin with one finger and at the same time dripping water into its mouth. The bird didn't seem to mind me touching it this way. After several attempts it worked. The bird was smart and came to understand that when I gently stroked its chin something would go into its mouth. Success was sweet.

Food was the next challenge. I soaked tiny crumbs of bread in water and put these in its mouth, later switching to milk. It was a hungry baby and I fed it often throughout the day. At night we closed the box up tight and left it until morning.

In the morning it was exciting to hear little cheeps, open the box, take our bird out and start the day with feeding. Very satisfying to note that this bird had pooped. Our cats were definitely interested but we made sure they didn't get near the box or even see our baby. In a few days the bird began to show signs of feathers. After a week or so it was covered in feathers and had grown little wings.

This young bird got restless. It began to fly up and hit the top of the closed box. I started taking it out of the box and putting it on our deck where it could practise flying. I put it on the railing of the deck and soon it was able to fly down to the deck floor and eventually back up again to the rail. The rail was a good place to feed it. I'd put crumbs out for it. It liked this idea. It was used to me and never seemed to mind my picking it up and putting it back in its box home. It was a handsome young bird, a sparrow. When it started singing at dawn what a happy triumph.

A sumac tree grew right up against the deck, thick with branches and leaves. It was just a hop from the rail. In the tree there were lots of little spiders. I thought that perhaps the bird might like to eat one of them. I tried putting it in the tree where it was easy for it to find a perch. It stayed in the tree for a while; however, when I put a crumb out on the rail, it flew back to eat. At night I continued to put it safely in its box home.

One day I put it in the tree and it didn't come back to the rail to feed. It stayed in the tree overnight. At dawn I was awake to hear the first birds singing. I listened and listened and was certain I recognized my bird's song, sure I knew its unique voice. When I went outside to check there it was on the rail waiting to be fed.

For a few more days it stayed out at night and I had the joy of hearing it sing in the morning. Then one morning our bird didn't come back. It was gone, finding its life amongst the trees with other sparrows.

Murray Harbour

Some places you just live in for a long or short time, while other places leave a lasting impression upon you. You can't tell exactly why. Somehow you found the right place at the right time. We lived in Murray Harbour on the White Sands Road for four years and in that time the Harbour gently wove its life around us and we were happy.

At least once on most days we walked a familiar route behind the house. First, down the field, then through a small wood, across a meadow, a short distance through a potato field and finally down a narrow swamp road. One could walk quite a distance on this road before it ended in wetness. In  spring the swamp came alive with every day bringing fresh growth. Brilliant marsh marigolds were the first blooms to appear, then came the ferns and grasses, a green paradise. In Maytime everyone talked of

 where to find mayflowers. On our swamp road they were in fragrant abundance—pink, and pink and white.

At the end of the road the tree branches formed a canopy. Here you could rest in the quiet beauty and listen to the white-throated sparrows singing to one another back and forth, back and

forth. In June lady slippers flourished in groups along our walking path. One day I counted eighty. In amongst the swamp rushes the wild purple irises shone.

On the way home one could return on the same pathway or avoid the potato field by taking a narrow shortcut from the swamp road through to the meadow. We did that the odd time, and once happened upon a nest of tiny newborn garter snakes, perhaps ten of them together, just babies.

In summer the meadow was alive with wild flowers: daisies, Queen Anne's lace, later the orange, white and yellow Indian paintbrush, multitudes of wild flowers. Asters and goldenrod foretold the fall. It was a procession of flowers—so many to know and name.

Our purebred collie Tess always went with us. In the woods there was a roundabout where she chased rabbits. They were fast and always got away. In fact they got to know her and played with her. One rabbit would run ahead while another watched her chasing from behind. Her ways with the rabbits didn't seem too smart but perhaps it was fun for all and Tess didn't really want to catch one, only herd them.

On another occasion she showed her collie breeding, definitely knowing how best to handle a possibly dangerous situation. My husband and I and Tess had walked as usual to the end of the swamp road. We began to hear the baying of hounds in the distance and then the voices got louder. They seemed to be coming our way so we headed for home. I was walking some way ahead of my husband and at the mouth of the road where it joined the potato field, when a coyote was suddenly there, no more than ten feet away from me. It was, a large healthy animal. I was stunned and still.

The coyote had obviously been running. It took a quick look

down the swamp road, made a decision not to go there, ran a short way along our route home, then stopped and took a huge leap into the swamp, perhaps seeking the firm ground of the smaller trail. Then it was gone.

A moment or two later along came two small hound dogs, baying in pursuit of the coyote. Tess had disappeared, gone home on our usual route. The dogs didn't stop. They followed the coyote scent as far as they could, then continued on, baying and following Tess's scent. They ended up at our home having lost the coyote completely. They did find Tess in the yard, seemed confused for a few moments, then away they went. Two smart animals, the collie and the coyote. Other animals used the swamp road, partridge and sometimes a fox. I hoped I wouldn't be so close to a coyote again.

So many vivid memories linger: seeing the lobster fishers at sunrise on their first morning, heading out of the harbour with horns blaring and lights flashing; enjoying delicious chowder at Brehaut's; being wakened on a moonlit night by a magnificent flock of at least two hundred wild geese flying directly overhead, honking and vibrating the air with their powerful wings. Wherever they were going it was important and you wanted to go with them.

One evening, returning to Murray Harbour after a day away, a warm feeling came to me and I realized that this place had become a true home, a home I seem to have lost over the years. And I was happy.

VOICES

Joanne Collicott McGuigan

Joanne lives with her husband Wayne and their cat Li'red a few kilometres south of Montague, Prince Edward Island.

Joanne considers herself not *from away*, but an *Islander by marriage*. Her husband's ancestors, Jack McGuigan and his wife Peggy Hughes, emigrated from County Monaghan, Ireland and arrived on Prince Edward Island around 1840. They settled in the St. Mary's Road area in Sturgeon.

Joanne feels it is exactly as Lucy Maude Montgomery, author of Anne of Green Gables once said, "Once you come to the Island you feel you have come home."

Joanne enjoys walking in the fresh air and listening to Celtic inspired music of the Maritimes. She loves feeding the multitude of blue jays, juncos, squirrels and two beautiful ravens that frequent her backyard.

The secrets of the mind as well as the universe and the betterment of mankind have always been important interests to her.

Two of the author's books available on Amazon are *Child of Danaan*, an account of Joanne's mystical journey after the sudden death of her only child and *The Dream Mechanism,* a compilation of dream analysis columns she wrote for an Ontario newspaper. She has also contributed short stories to the first two anthologies by the Montague Library Writers Guild.

Joanne mainly writes documentaries and true stories. She hopes to expand upon the story included here. In researching the story of Minnie McGee she relied on numerous sources including newspaper accounts and interviews with several area residents. She would like to thank them for their insights.

Joanne may be contacted at: redheadpei@yahoo.ca

VOICES

The Tragedy of Minnie McGee

In the fourth month of the year 1912 the nation was shocked as the news swept across the land of the unsinkable RMS Titanic having hit an iceberg in the frigid waters of the North Atlantic Ocean. The lives of hundreds of passengers were needlessly lost because of a shortage of lifeboats. At the same time residents on the beautiful red shores of the Canadian Island of Prince Edward were mourning the mysterious deaths of five children and would soon also mourn the death of the family's last remaining child.

Details of these two compelling tragedies were published on the same day, April 19, 1912, in the Charlottetown Patriot newspaper. They had listed the death toll from the Titanic as 1,601. On the same page is an article about the puzzling deaths of the McGee children. The headline read; *The only remaining child Johnny is now ill-Having the same symptoms as the other five.*

In the early 1900's life could be depressing for the average person on Prince Edward Island. There was much strenuous hard work with little compensation. It was a constant struggle to meet the family needs. Often there was no foreseeable future of anything better. Even so, one has to question the mental state of Minnie Cassidy McGee when after poisoning her children she said at her trial, "I dearly loved the children but thought they would be better off in heaven."

At the time of Minnie's trial the population of Prince Edward Island was 93,728. The province was divided between Catholic and

Joanne Collicott McGuigan: The Tragedy of Minnie McGee

Protestant affiliations. No matter what religion they were, the residents of the tiny Canadian Island pondered on the breaking of the sacred trust existing between a mother and her child. In this case it was not one but six precious children who had lost their lives because their mother could not control the persistent voice in the dark recesses of her mind calling for the deaths of her children. Minnie had told Constable McKearney that the idea of killing her children haunted her day and night. In a written confession Minnie admitted that she gave her six children the ends of matches in weak tea and sugar and intended to kill herself as well.

The Island Patriot reports in a small column of the paper, Saturday, April 27, 1912:

Arrest of Mrs. McGee
She Was Remanded for Trial Next Thursday at Georgetown.

Mrs Patrick McGee of St. Mary's Road, one of the chief witnesses in the recent investigations into the death by poisoning of her six children, has been arrested yesterday afternoon by Constables McCarron and McKearney and taken to the King's County Jail at Georgetown. She was taken before Mr. J. H. Reddin, Stipendiary Magistrate for King's County, and remanded until Thursday next at 11 o'clock. It is expected that before the trial opens next Thursday a report will have been received from Provincial Health Officer MacMillan, now in Montreal inspecting the chemical analysis of the contents of the stomach and certain organs of the deceased children. Mrs. McGee took her arrest quite coolly and did not seem to be greatly exercised over the situation. It is understood that there was a desire on the part of the people of the locality that Mrs. McGee should be placed in safekeeping until the mystery was further sifted. The charge that was formally laid against her is that of murder in the case of the last boy Johnny."

The newspaper report was met with total astonishment when it became apparent Minnie had orchestrated the deaths of her own children. People wondered how one could do this monstrous thing. Minnie was known as a rather odd person and the last three years she was rarely seen outside her home. Others said it must be the fault of her husband. He was rarely home and when he was, he treated her badly.

VOICES

Testimonies at Minnie's Trial. Testifying at Minnie's trial in Georgetown were the owners of the stores where the deadly matches were bought, Mrs. William Hicken and Annie Mahar. At that time you could get over a hundred matches for one cent. Clerks at the store testified her grocery orders included large numbers of matches. In her testimony Minnie denied she had placed orders with the stores so she could stockpile matches in the weeks preceding April 11. The Tuesday before he died, Johnny the last remaining child had gone to Hicken's store at Commercial Road Crossing and purchased four cents worth of matches, a pair of stockings and a piece of candy.

In addition there were testimonies from Minnie's father, Thomas Cassidy and her brothers, Ambrose and Peter. Her cousins, Robert and Thomas McCarron and her neighbours, Edward McGuigan, Peter Gormley and Ellen McGuigan also testified. Ambrose Cassidy's evidence was mainly about an earlier conversation he had with Bailiff McCarron. There had been suspicions that Minnie was responsible for having burned down a barn belonging to Ambrose. Ambrose said he had never charged his sister with setting fire to the barn and a hay stack. Her father testified he had thought of having her institutionalized a few years before. All the other witnesses, with the exception of Ellen McGuigan, told of strange actions by the prisoner as well as threats uttered by her to do terrible things.

Edward McGuigan, a neighbour of the McGee's, testified Minnie had said on the day Johnny was ill that she was going away somewhere. She intended to leave her husband Pat anyway and said that he could get married again. She said the thirteen years of her married life were years thrown away. Minnie was blaming Johnny's sickness on candy purchased at Hicken's store and on spoiled herring for the demise of the other children.

Minnie's reply at her hearing on July 22, 1912:

"*Take mercy on me I have had a hard life. In January my head went all astray and worse in February and worse in April. Pain in my head right through away in there. This last four months pain was dreadful I was going to do away with my own life. I cannot do away with the pain in my head. Before I would be sick Pat McGee would beat me, and when*

Joanne Collicott McGuigan: The Tragedy of Minnie McGee

I would get sick he would beat me in bed. He would not get me a drink, said I could stay there until I rotted. He would go around and say he was going to shoot himself. There is a pain in my head goes right through, I don't know what is the matter with it, I am tired of that pain. Just as soon do away with my own life. Terrible pain in my head. He could have taken the children away. He had four months warning. It was his fault, not mine. It is all his fault. I dearly loved the children."

When giving her testimony about the circumstances surrounding the deaths of her children it was reported that Minnie wept bitterly at times and talked in a rambling way. Her evidence on the whole was most unsatisfactory. Minnie's husband, Pat McGee, was called to the stand. On cross-examination by the Attorney General he contradicted several statements made by her.

Mr. Justice FitzGerald ruled that the hanging of Minnie McGee take place on October 10th at Georgetown. This made Minnie the first woman in Prince Edward Island to have the death sentence imposed upon her. The jury had recommended mercy. There was public sympathy because of her gender and her condition in life.

Upon hearing her first sentence of death by hanging pronounced Minnie's hysterical reply was, "Hang me, hang me, hang me now and be done with it! Hang me right here in the box!"

The close-knit neighbourhood of St. Mary's Road was sent reeling when Minnie became a suspect and was subsequently sentenced to hang. It was especially hard for the people involved, the constables McCarron and McKearney and the many neighbours, including John, Edward and Steve McGuigan, Tom Murphy and Michael Gormley, who had come to the McGee house to try and help when the children became ill. Each neighbour wondered if somehow the tragedy could have been prevented if Minnie had had more support to help her through her troubles, or with the poisoning of the mind, which had worsened with the negative thoughts she entertained daily. Were the deaths of her two youngest children in January the final catalyst to have sent Minnie over the brink?

A petition was sent by her neighbours to spare her life pleading that she be committed to an insane asylum. Her death sentence was later changed to life imprisonment. In 1912 courts did not grant leniency to the mentally disturbed. The never ending pain in her head combined with the constant urges to kill her children four months prior to doing so indicate she had a severe disorder. The field of psychoanalysis was in its infancy. The medical field had no knowledge of complications from post partum depression (PPD) and the deadly turn it can take if not treated.

Deaths of the children. The timeline for the deaths of the children started with Minnie, Pat and five of their six children sitting down to a meal on Thursday, April 11, 1912. The children; Louis, Pansy, George, Bridget and Thomas gathered around the table and eagerly devoured the dinner of herring, potatoes and tea. Soon afterwards the children became ill and one by one, over the course of the next couple days, passed away. Pat was not affected but Minnie was reported to have been sick and to have vomited twice.

The children appeared to get drowsy and some complained of pains around their hearts. All the children were sick to their stomachs and had vomited. Thirteen-year-old Louis seemed to be in the most discomfort, rolling and groaning on the bed. He and six-year-old Bridget were the first to die. Twelve-year-old Pansy had a bluish tinge around her lips and she complained of a slight pain in her limbs. Within two days after the family meal on April 11, Pansy, eight-year-old George and five-year-old Thomas slowly succumbed to the poison in their systems.

The children's burial was Sunday, April 14, the day after the fifth child died. One child, Johnny, was visiting his uncle, Ambrose Cassidy. He was not at home for the fatal dosage but returned home after the funeral of his siblings. By Tuesday he had taken ill. The doctors examined him on Thursday at the McGee

Mrs. McGee and Johnny after the funeral

home but Johnny passed away that night.

Unlikely as it would be expected of someone who had lost one child, much less five, Pat went to work at Hewitt's Lobster Factory in Sturgeon the Monday after the funeral of his five children, leaving Johnny in Minnie's care. From St. Mary's Road east to Sturgeon would have been a fair distance to walk and would have been made even harder by the shocking burden of sorrow and uncertainty he must have carried. At Minnie's trial Pat testified he was afraid to go to work as she might poison his last remaining child. He said Minnie told him to go and he went because, as he said, "I was not the boss." The newspaper articles referred to Pat as a hardworking farmer. He is listed as a fisherman in the 1911 census. Although he was home at the time of the poisoning of the first five children he was away a good deal of the time, perhaps looking for other employment when there wasn't any fishing. Pat McGee was also very much a victim in this tragedy. He lost his entire family. His life would be forever clouded by the suspicions he had abused his wife, therefore not a lot of sympathy was extended to him.

The Doctors who attended the Children.

In 1912, travelling required time and was generally uncomfortable. Horses played a huge role in everyday life. The doctors who attended the McGee children had to travel by horseback or horse and buggy over narrow dirt roads and swampy grounds in rain or shine. The automobile had been invented but they were banned on PEI from 1908 until 1913 mainly because the noise scared the horses. It would have been an approximate distance of about ten kilometers, or about six miles, from Montague to the McGee house on St. Mary's Road.

Montague, then a village of about nine hundred people, did have some telephone service but because of the lack of phones in the countryside it would be a while before word would get through to a doctor to check in on the sick.

At the time of the McGee family tragedy there were two doctors practising medicine in Montague, Dr. David Fraser and Dr. John MacIntyre. Intermittently, both of these doctors had been at the McGee house when the children were sick and dying. They administered medicines but were helpless to stop the deaths. They suspected poison but did not know what kind. At first it was thought ptomaine poisoning from the fish the family had eaten was the cause. This was a puzzle to the doctors as the children did not have all the symptoms associated with eating decaying fish. The sick ones were complaining of pains in their heads and stomachs and had vomited green matter. There was no movement of the bowels and that fact seemed peculiar in view of the other symptoms. When the remaining child, ten-year-old Johnny, exhibited the same ailments that had taken the lives of the other five children Dr. Fraser became suspicious that something was amiss. The week before the doctor had thought Minnie was not acting in the character as a grieving mother when she started mopping the kitchen floor while he was attending to her children as they lay groaning in pain. She was acting strangely and talking irrationally at times.

He knew people have different ways of handling stress but when Johnny became ill and Minnie was acting in the same cold unresponsive manner it was a red flag to the young doctor. He got permission from the authorities to remove Johnny from the McGee home. The two doctors found it unsettling when this petite, bony woman railed at them as they tried to prepare her son to be taken out of the house. Minnie ranted and raved and stamped her feet when they removed Johnny from her questionable care to her father's safekeeping. The move to Thomas Cassidy's home came too late. The poison had already done its work and Johnny died at his grandfather's that night.

The Marriage of Minnie Cassidy and Patrick McGee.

Minnie's married life started in the fall of 1898 on lot 61, St. Mary's Road, King's County, Prince Edward Island. She was twenty-one at the time. Minnie was born February 4, 1877 and given the name Mary Elizabeth Cassidy; Patrick's birth date was October 12, 1873. In the marriage register at St. Paul's Church, Sturgeon, there is recorded a marriage between Patrick McGee and Mary Cassidy on November 15, 1898. The witnesses to their wedding were Christopher Lafferty and Flora Cassidy. Flora may have been a nickname for Minnie's younger sister, Florence.

Minnie Cassidy and Patrick (or Pat as he was called) McGee

were both of Irish descent and Roman Catholic faith. Cassidy is an Irish surname anglicized from the Gaelic origin O'Caiside. Around 1840 both Minnie and Patrick's grandparents would have leased land on Prince Edward Island from absentee British landlords and may have followed the same treacherous crossing of the North Atlantic as the route taken by the unfortunate passenger liner RMS Titanic. Most of the Irish emigrants on St. Mary's Road came from County Armagh or County Monaghan having left Ireland just before the great famine. Many in Minnie's time could still speak the Irish Gaelic.

Minnie was about fifteen years old when her mother Bridget died after giving birth to baby Edward who also succumbed. As the eldest child in the Cassidy household Minnie was not a stranger to illness, death and sorrow. At a young age she witnessed the passing of four children her mother had lost, either at birth or under two years of age. Her father Thomas Cassidy worked as a mail driver. Minnie would have taken on the role as caregiver to help her father raise her six younger brothers and sisters; Peter, Florence, Lucy A, Thomas, Ambrose and Rose E.

Even in difficult times, after prayers on the rosary were said each evening, the squawk of the fiddle and singing and dancing could be heard coming from numerous houses along St. Mary's Road. Minnie liked to step dance and, no doubt, in a happier state of mind would relate to her own children all those delightful stories of the magical little people, fairies and ghostly apparitions she and heard in her childhood.

Louis was born to Minnie in 1898. He was the first of her nine children.

The two youngest, Mary and Clara died in January, 1912. About a year earlier, Albert, a three-year-old, had passed. Minnie had threatened her family and husband after the deaths of her two youngest children in January. She would fly into uncontrollable rages at the smallest provocations. She expressed concern that she may do something to her six remaining children and wanted them taken away. Her father and the few people close to her worried about what she might do but they did not think she would harm the children. However, in light of what happened to the six remaining children the previous deaths also came under question. Therefore the bodies of the younger children were exhumed and tested. It was confirmed they had died of whooping cough and pneumonia.

No one knows what really goes on in a marriage except for the two involved. There was a lot of speculation when Minnie said that besides beating her Pat went around saying he was going to shoot himself. Does this point to his exasperation in dealing with his wife's worsening mental state? The beatings she received would only have compounded her condition. Any feelings of affection towards him would have soured and being the feisty woman she was, turned to thoughts of revenge. From all reports, Minnie did not suffer fools gladly and was of the mindset 'wrong me and I will pay you back'. She indicated she wanted to leave her husband but this would have been nearly impossible in 1912. A wife was still thought of as the property of her husband and too often was the victim of domestic violence from a husband who thought this was a way to keep her in line. The poison was not fed to him but was planned for her and the children to go to a better place. Perhaps she thought they could all join her three other deceased children in heaven. In her fragile state of mind was leaving Pat alone to suffer the loss of his family going to be her ultimate revenge?

The ground where Minnie's house stood on St. Mary's Road is a few blocks from the corner of Commercial Road. Today, all that is left of it is a sunken hole in the ground on beautifully landscaped property owned by Vincent and Sandra McCarthy. The now vacant lot lies peacefully between the McCarthy house and their neighbour, Gary McGuigan. The original house was a two-storey structure, rather small, with two bedrooms and a kitchen on the main floor and sleeping quarters in the loft. Sandra gave me copies of 1912 newspaper reports on Minnie's trial. These reports were most helpful in my research on what lead to a housewife and mother poisoning her beloved children.

Current Conversations Regarding the Tragedy. A descendant of one of St. Mary's Road original families, Vonda McGuigan Loane, remembers stories told of the sadness felt throughout the community as two teams of horses pulled the wagons carrying the five white coffins to St. Paul's graveyard. Minnie and Pat had the sympathies and prayers of the whole congregation as Minnie and her last remaining child, Johnny, forlornly stood beside the freshly dug gravesite of her five children. Little did anyone attending the burial realize this would be the last time they would see Johnny alive. Vonda had heard Minnie  was an excellent seamstress and had heard that the clothes the children were wearing as they lay in their coffins had been made by her not long before.

I spent an afternoon with Vonda checking the grounds where Minnie's house stood and then searching St. Paul's cemetery. We found the weathered gravestone of the McGee children. On the stone the names of the children and their ages are listed as;

Louise 13,
Penzie 12,
Johnie 10,
George 8,
Bridget 6,
Thomas 5.
Children of Patrick & Minnie MacGee.

There are some inconsistencies on the gravestone. For example, the oldest child's name was Louis not Louise and Penzie was perhaps a nickname for Penelope who was also sometimes called Pansy. The name McGee is misspelled MacGee.

Edna Daly Graham had worked at Falconwood Asylum in Charlottetown where Minnie was confined. Edna's son, Hughie Graham, of Whim Road in Sturgeon related the story of his mother shaking a finger at her and Minnie trying to bite the finger. His grandmother never forgot the heartbreaking image of the children's caskets laid out in the apple orchard before transported to their final resting place in St. Paul's cemetery.

Hughie said there was a play performed in the early 1980's at the King's Playhouse in Georgetown. It was a supposedly true story of a downtrodden Island woman who poisoned her six children. It upset the relatives and neighours of the families involved and was eventually cancelled. Many people thought the play did not represent the actual facts of the case. Someone involved in the production of the play had asked his mother what Minnie looked like. Hughie said he did not pay much attention at the time but remembers his mother saying Minnie wore her hair tied back loosely in a bun. The newspaper articles stated she was pale and thin at her trial. She has been described as a tiny bony woman with dark hair and deep-set brown eyes. The community didn't blame Minnie entirely for the murders of her six children. They thought she must have been crazy to commit such a terrible thing and that she should have been placed in an insane asylum. I asked Hughie about Minnie's husband, Patrick McGee, and he said he wasn't thought too much of around these parts after the story broke and he had heard he left this area and died in Nova Scotia years later.

Hughie mentioned that an important consequence of this tragedy was that the Eddy Match Company eventually reduced the content of sulphur and phosphorus used in matches. Not only Minnie but other people had used the heads of matches to kill. Minnie had broken the blue heads off the matches, soaked the ends in weak tea, added sugar and had given this mixture to her children to drink. Twenty-five to thirty-five of these phosphorus match heads would be a fatal dose for an adult.

Both Hughie and Vonda spoke of hearing about a doctor and his wife who had thought highly of Minnie and even had her take care of their children. I later found out this to be a Dr. Murchison. The laneway into Hillsborough Hospital and Special Care Centre is named after him.

Preston McGuigan's family resided in the St. Mary's Road area when the McGee children passed away. He shed some light on the question of how Minnie knew the ends of the matches would have ingredients powerful enough to poison someone. As a child he was always told not to put the matches in his mouth as they would kill you. When you struck one there was a loud bang and a huge flame.

Preston remembered his father Philip talking about the tragic death of the McGee children. Philip, a young boy at the time, was the first on the scene when the last child, Johnny, became ill. Philip ran home as fast as his legs could go to get help. When the neighbours came and tried to revive Johnny, Minnie came forward with a glass of something that looked like milk.

She said, "Here give him this to drink, it will help him."

One of the men replied, "You drink it yourself."

But she did not drink whatever was in the glass.

Preston said as a child he was afraid to venture into the woods surrounding the McGee homestead and would go out of his way to avoid the area. Because he had heard spirits could not cross water he always travelled on the opposite side of the brook that flowed behind the homestead. There had been a house and a barn still standing when he was a youngster. Only hearing bits and pieces of the tragedy and not realizing Minnie was confined, Preston and other local children thought she was still lurking around waiting for a chance to grab them. Many an evening, safely gathered around the warm dancing fire in the old wood store he would sit on the floor wide-eyed and spellbound listening to the frightening stories his older brother loved to embellish. One was about hearing the rustling of footsteps in the leaves behind him as he walked through the property in the fall. He could hear what sounded like deep breathing and was sure someone was close behind him but on turning around, no one was there. Other stories of the woods were the sightings of six rabbits, six crows or six ducks representing the children.

Preston remembered a little skipping ditty they would sing as going something like this:

"*Minnie McGee, she poisoned me,*
She put matches in my tea."

Falconwood Asylum. After her conviction Minnie was incarcerated in penitentiaries at Kingston, Ontario and Dorchester, New Brunswick before returning to Charlottetown in 1928. The Falconwood Asylum where Minnie was housed burned in December 1931. Falconwood was rebuilt in 1933 and in 1957 was renamed Riverside Hospital. An additional building, Hillsborough Hospital, was added and remains on the site today at 115 Murchison Lane, Charlottetown. Today it is called Hillsborough Hospital and Special Care Centre. It is a peaceful park-like setting bordering on the Hillsborough River. On November 6, 2012, a friend, Connie Beaton Stewart, accompanied me into the Special Care Centre to see if I could retrieve any information about Minnie and her years there when it was Falconwood Insane Asylum. I was hoping to find out what kind of treatment Minnie received. We spoke with David Berrigan, Manager of Administration and Finance. He was unable to let me see any records but he was willing to talk about Minnie and what he had heard about her being institutionalized there. He recalled the skipping rhyme and heard from a retired worker that Minnie was quite grumpy and cantankerous the last few years before her death. This made me laugh as, by all accounts, she was that way all her life.

There was a Dr. Murchison administrating at the hospital from 1934 to 1962. His wife took Minnie under her wing and often had her doing tasks. Although the Doctor's wife did not work at the asylum she had training in psychoanalysis and thought what happened to Minnie was the result of post partum depression. This illness is not to be confused with 'baby blues' which some women experience a few days after giving birth. Baby blues is usually temporary and is believed to be caused by the hormonal changes taking place. If a new mother is still depressed and suffering symptoms a month or so after having a baby then she could be suffering post partum depression (PPD).

PPD can put a mother in a very dark place and if not diagnosed can lead to mental instability. In severe cases the person might hear an abusive and demanding voice telling them to harm their children or themselves. As a result the person can become isolated and withdrawn. It can be even more severe if there are already underlying problems such as a difficult birth, an unsympathetic partner, stress, money troubles or sad memories stirred up about the loss of loved ones.

Sandra King Stephens, Sturgeon, in going through some old

pictures found two of Minnie which she graciously lent me. One is Minnie with her son Johnny. In the other Minnie is front and center with some nurses on the grounds of Falconwood. Although the one of Minnie and Johnny is not of good quality it will give the reader an idea of what Minnie looked like at the time she buried her children. The picture is testimony to her skill as a seamstress when one looks at the two-piece suit she is wearing and the cute outfit on Johnny.

Minnie, in later life, situated in the middle (front row) of the nurses at Falconwood.

In 1933, after some twenty years of confinement, Minnie was allowed to return to her ailing father's home to care for him. The neighbours were afraid of what she might do and after his death so she was returned to Falconwood where she spent the last twenty years of her life. After spending time with her father she was much more reconciled to the circumstances surrounding the loss of her children, although the sadness never left her.

Minnie was not buried with her children but instead was interred in the Charlottetown Roman Catholic Church Cemetery. Her obituary appeared in the Guardian newspaper on January 8, 1953. In her seventy-sixth year, Minnie had lived some forty years with the knowledge of what she had done. At times she was inconsolable.

There was some good to come out of the April, 1912 tragedies.

The public outrage over the lack of sufficient lifeboats on the Titanic was instrumental in new maritime safety regulations being put in place. The International Convention for the Safety of Life at Sea was formed.

VOICES

Eddy Match Company eventually decreased the sulphur and phosphorus used in matches. Not only Minnie Cassidy McGee but others had used the heads of the matches for poison.

In April of this year, 2014, it will be one hundred and two years since the horrendous loss of lives from the Titanic shipwreck and the death of six innocent children at the hands of a mother suffering from what appears to be severe post partum depression. Their lives are not forgotten as the stories have been revisited and remembered over the years.

The Irish poet, William Butler Yeats wrote:

> *"Come away, O human child,*
> *to the waters and the wild,*
> *with a fairy, hand in hand,*
> *for the world is more full of weeping*
> *than you can understand."*

Blanche Moyaert

Blanche was born in the tobacco growing region of Southern Ontario. At the age of eight she became an 'Islander' when her family moved to a farm on Prince Edward Island. She attended school in Montague then went on to university 'off Island'.

At an early age she learned the love of books from her mother. She enjoyed writing rhymes and stories about friends and school experiences and faithfully kept a diary. During high school she accumulated over twenty pen pals. After graduating from university Blanche returned to the haven of PEI and back to hometown friends and family. During the busy years of marriage and children, bedtime stories composed on the spot were her main compositions and her journal-writing continued in fits and starts.

Since 1995 she has lived and worked in a number of different countries. Islanders always come home, they say. Blanche has returned and is remembering what it means to be *an Islander*.

Becoming an Islander

The following are excerpts from her soon to be published book, **'Becoming an Islander'** – *a story of the 1960's and her first years learning to be an Islander.*

VOICES

Three Score (and more).

At life's opening a big stone house in Southern Ontario,
a multihued society,
then a long drive with everything we own on the back of a truck,
a ferryboat ride
to an old whitewashed wooden farmhouse,
diamond-studded snow up to the telephone lines –
and a bear that wasn't a bear –
long country summers,
green fields, red clay roads and a horizon of blue sea and blue sky
School life where I could never be 'an Islander'…

Away to university 'off Island',
Frosh week, new friends, new found ideas –
a break for travel and love and finding out who I am –
on to a new found land, a rugged land of rising rocks and
    northwest winds,
graduation and teaching,
back to the Island,
contented years of Montessori School, Sesame Street, storytelling,
    hugs and tears.
Divorce …

Off to see the wide world with four kids in tow,
golden days in the African sun,
gray Belgium where I too meet Napoleon's Waterloo,
on to the silver city of the Weimar Republic
and the blackness of Buchenwald concentration camp,
then home to my Flemish roots,
KULeuven founded before Columbus 'found 'America,
the stunning 'stadhuis',
Flanders Fields where the poppies no longer blow.
Now full circle to the red clay isle
and not yet an Islander…

Blanche Moyaert: Becoming an Islander

Arrival . *Author's note: It is February, 1961. I'm eight years old. After three days driving from Ontario and a midnight ferry boat ride, we finally arrive on PEI. I have fallen asleep during the drive from 'the boat'.*

The next thing I remember is waking up in the dark as we arrived at the farm. The lane to the house was filled with snow higher than the car. We struggled over the snow banks to the house and dug out the kitchen door only to find that the door was locked. Having no key to the house, my dad managed to open the half-frozen window and shove my brother in with a flashlight to open the latch from the inside.

Inside all was frozen cold and absolutely dark. No electricity, no central heating, no indoor plumping, no telephone. It was quite a comedown from the modern government house we had left in Ontario. The first order of business was to light the oil lamps – full of oil, domes cleaned, wicks primed sitting on the kitchen table with a box of 'strike anywhere' matches beside them ready to go. Next, to kindle the fire in the wood stove. The wood had also been nicely laid needing only a match to be ignited. A friendly neighbour had laid all in preparation for our arrival. I remember the greasy smell of the oil lamp as it flickered and burned in contrast to the woodsy aroma of the wood fire as it crackled and burned. Both odours were new to me but even so, very homey and welcoming. Amidst this activity I heard the jingle of bells from outside, then a knock at the door. Everyone else was engaged and I appeared to be the only one aware of this knocking so I opened the door. There stood a tall fur-clad figure covered with snow. I screamed!

"*A bear!*"

It was the first introduction to our closest neighbour, Long Dan MacDonald. We could see his farm on the hill a quarter mile to the west. We later found out that just like Old MacDonald's Farm of 'e-i-e-i-o' fame, his farm had all the animals found in the song. In later months the cacophony of the farm animals would become a familiar sound across the fields. On this winter early morning he had been watching for the light in the window and had hitched up his horse and sleigh to come over to welcome us and see if there was anything we needed. His wife Miny had packed a lunch for us in anticipation since she realized there would be no ready food in the house for a family with three small children.

I was quite relieved to see 'the bear' disrobe and to realize that he was human after all.

She Sees Me. *Author's note: Long Dan's wife would later become an important friend to me.*

They laugh at me when
I say she's my best friend.
With grownup sons she's too old
And she's blind.
But I love her more than any other friend.

She was gone for a long time, away,
"To get her eyes fixed" they say.
And now she wants to see me.
To see me!

Mama curls my hair
And adds a beautiful blue bow
To match my Sunday best dress.
But still I'm afraid.

"Come near me, Child," she says,
"I want to see you."
She sees me.

"You look exactly like I thought."
She smiles.

A Time. One evening we were all in the kitchen when we heard voices outside. I ran to the window and saw lanterns and flashlights bobbing up the lane toward the house. Who was this coming? We didn't know that our neighbours had planned 'a time' to welcome us to the community. Earlier in the week, one neighbour had checked that we would be home that day. All seven families from Head of Montague, a few folks from neighbouring Lyndale on one side and

Victoria Cross on the other had been notified of the time and date. No other organization was needed, for traditionally everyone knew what to do. The women brought baked goods – cakes, sweet squares and little tuna, ham and chicken salad sandwiches with the crusts cut off, fruit drinks and, of course, tea - a most important contribution expected by all. Coffee had not really entered the culture. Only people from 'away' drank coffee.

I didn't know it at the time but there was something else going on out of sight. Bottles of moonshine, whisky and other such drinks were being stashed away in the barn. Prohibition on the Island had long ended but the attitudes of the temperance movement were still very active. Drinking alcohol in public was not socially acceptable so those who wished to imbibe (in all cases only men) slipped out to the barn and returned later socially lubricated for dancing, singing and stomping to the music.

I stood in the corner completely overwhelmed by this invasion. For invasion it was. Coats were carried upstairs and thrown on the beds. A group of chattering women took over the pantry and started organizing the food. A few young men pushed the table into the middle of the kitchen and lined the chairs up against the wall facing into the center. The livingroom doors were flung open and furniture pushed into the corners. The oil stove was lit to take the frigid edge off the air while the carpet was rolled up to make room for a dance floor.

The musicians, local farmers from the neighbourhood, started to tune up their fiddles and guitars. I later became familiar with the sound of instrument tuning heard at all the local 'times' and concerts. Ping, ping, strum. Turn the little knobs on the strings, ping, ping. "That's better." Strum, strum. When the players were satisfied that they were all tuned to the same key, they began playing short snatches of tunes together. This was the only rehearsal needed for a whole night of music and dancing.

Then it began. The music played in earnest. I watched in fascination. Without any direction people started to form a square. One couple stood in the center floor holding hands and tapping toes in time to the music. Soon another stood facing them and two more couples joined at either side forming the square. On a musical cue, the dancing started. Old and young, anyone could dance. Most couples were a man and woman or a boy and girl, but it was quite common for two girls to dance together although it was not for two boys.

The traditional square dance originated with the English, Irish, Scottish and French ancestors of today's Islanders. In this 'old time square dance' no caller is needed. The simple movements are well known with the head couple leading. Head couples back and forth, side couples back and forth, swing your corner, swing your partner. You often keep changing partners until you return to your original partner and the 'set' is over.

But this would not do for long as more than four couples wanted to dance. As many people as could fit in the available space holding hands in a circle joined for a round dance. A newcomer can easily join in without lessons by following the lead of the person ahead of them in the chain. The person behind also can give a friendly nudge in the right direction.

Everyone joins hands in circling to the right and then to the left, then all into the center with raised arms and a big cheer, out to swing your partner. Then grand chain, ladies moving to the left and gentlemen to the right, right hand to right hand, left to left until you meet your own partner again. Arm in arm as in a waltz, right foot pointed into the center as a pivot, swing round and round. It could take your breath away! The men were often in competition to see who could swing their partner the longest. The others would clap and stomp in time to the music encouraging and cheering on the swinging couples.

Then there were line dances where partners faced each other in a line and weaved in and out, back to back, doing the do-si-do. The couple at the head of the line, leading the way, split the pairs into two lines – ladies one way and gents the other, curving around and meeting at the bottom end again where the head couple forms an arch by joining hands. Each pair, taking the hand of their partner, skips under the arch and forms two lines once more facing each other. Now we had the same movements with a new head couple. The music continued until all couples had the opportunity to be head couple.

There was a little break for the musicians to "whet their whistles" and to "get a bit of nourishment" before the next set. My brother was running around with the neighbour boys. They had found a space in the back porch to play marbles since they were not interested in the dancing. They were interested in eating however and upon hearing the word 'food' they were the first in line and now all four sat on the floor in the porch with plates of 'goodies' beside them. "Go get something to eat!" they called. I had no real interest in joining them. I couldn't wait for the dancing to start again.

I heard the tuning up begin. A neighbour, the son of Long Dan MacDonald (the same Long Dan who had so frightened me disguised as a bear) took me by the hand - a grownup man and me a very little girl – and pulled me into the dance circle.

"I don't know what to do." I cried.

A friendly female voice next to me said, "Just follow me, dear."

On the other side a second said, "I'll poke you when you have to move."

The dancing started. In and out, round and round. True to her word, lady #2 took me by the shoulders and steered me in the right direction. This wasn't so hard. But then came the swinging. My tall laughing partner picked me off my feet and swung me round and round. I finally landed so dizzy I couldn't walk.

I remember that night going on and on. I became a more and

more proficient dancer. It was past midnight when my father came to me and said that it was so late and I should go to bed. I was pleasantly exhausted but hesitant that I might miss more fun. I wearily crawled up the stairs and into bed. Still I could plainly hear the happy sounds from the living room below. I couldn't resist knowing what was going on downstairs. The stove pipe from the oil stove below heated my room as it went through on its way to the chimney. Through the grate I caught glimpses of the dancers and people milling around.

Gradually it quieted down. First the music stopped and the instruments were packed up. The floor was swept and the carpet replaced. The furniture returned to its proper place. It was nearly 4 am. As I began to lose interest my head began to nod. It found its way back to its pillow.

Late the next day I wandered downstairs to the kitchen. Everything was 'spic and span'. Everything was in order. It was as if the night before had not happened. Had it been a dream? Later, when I stepped outside to go to the barn, the telltale sleigh tracks and trampled snow were clear evidence of the reality of the night before.

This was my first 'time', a tradition on Prince Edward Island where the culture was still community-based in the 1960's. I experienced many similar events later. I came to know what to expect whenever we got word that we were going to a time at somebody's house for their anniversary or birthday or other special event. But little did I know that this tradition would not last much longer.

The 'old fashioned time' may be just that – old fashioned and out-of-date. But I have many enjoyable memories of those community times.

Winter. *Author's note: It was winter, going into spring, before my brother and I started going to school. Not just winter but the worst winter in twenty years. We had never seen snow like this.*

One Sunday Mama called us to get up for church. A jug of water stood beside a basin on the dresser in my bedroom with a facecloth and bar of soap in a dish to the other side. A hand towel hung ready on a rack on the side of the dresser. A chamber pot had been slid under the bed.

Blanche Moyaert: Becoming an Islander

"Don't forget to wash before getting dressed for church." came my mother's voice at the bottom of the stairs. The expectation was that each of us would wash our face, ears, neck and underarms from within our nightclothes trying to maintain the body heat generated during the night.

"Yes, Mama." I answered.

That morning it was so cold that I had to break a thin layer of ice before pouring the water into the basin. Gingerly I wet the cloth, dabbed my face and neck, not daring to disturb the warmth within my pyjamas. I hung the wet washcloth up to dry. Mama would check that the washcloth had been used.

Grabbing my Sunday best clothes I raced downstairs to the warmth of the kitchen to dress in front of the friendly wood stove's open oven door. Daddy was always the first one up early to rekindle the stove which, although stoked to capacity before going to bed, was usually reduced to a bed of warm coals by morning. This particular Sunday morning he had already gone out to dig out the driveway and get the car ready to drive the five miles to church. A few minutes later Daddy came in stomping and shaking off the snow. He told us to go back to bed for we weren't going to church that morning after all. Why? He couldn't find the car! It was completely covered by snow. I ran up the stairs to look down from the bedroom window. I could barely recognize the tip of the radio aerial where the car had been left last night.

Prince Edward Island was certainly a 'Winter Wonderland'.

VOICES

***Different*.** It was when I was eight years old that I felt different for the first time. In Ontario I had left a diverse immigrant community. No one there felt different because *everyone* was a bit different.

Montague Memorial School had eight classrooms with one grade per classroom which was a new experience for me. I had always attended mixed-age classes. Among the 35 children in our classroom I was the only one from 'away'. It was late in the school year and my grade three classmates all knew each other very well. Not only was this their third year together, but everyone seemed to be related. Everyone except for me had cousins in the classroom. Their families were all friends and neighbours and many knew each other from church and Sunday school. I was the only 'stranger'. I could see many eyes watching me. I seemed to be quite entertaining no matter what I did. Back in Ontario with our Belgian relatives we had all spoken a mixture of English and Flemish. Sometimes there were things I couldn't say in English. These special words or phrases I inserted naturally into my speech. But when this happened in school there was an explosion of laughter. Even the teacher couldn't help laughing. I have never in my life felt so ashamed. But the worst was that I didn't know why they were all laughing at me.

It was a custom in Belgian families to pierce the ears of baby girls. I had worn earrings, day and night since I was two months old. To me they were just a part of my body. I never removed them to wash, to sleep or anything. A couple of boys in the class teased me incessantly about these earrings calling out, "Mrs. Blanche is an old married woman." In their minds only married women wore earrings.

My clothes were also odd. I wore the hand-me-downs of my mother's sister, an aunt who was only nine years older than me. She had been like a big sister to me and these clothes reminded me of Aunt Jeanette whom I missed very much. In my eyes they were beautiful – fancy, flouncy ruffles and swishy satiny skirts with crinolines and frilly, lacy blouses. Many of these fine clothes had come from Flanders, noted for its textiles and lace work. But they were very unlike the plaid wool skirts and hand knitted sweaters of my classmates. "*Movie star!*" they jeered at me.

But the worst thing was my shoes. Because I had problems with my feet I wore special heavy orthopedic walking shoes. They were very expensive and we could afford only one pair. I had to wear them all the time. The doctor had solemnly told me, "If you don't wear your shoes everyday your legs will grow crooked and you will end up in a wheelchair."

The school rule was that outdoor footwear must be removed at the clothes rack and indoor shoes left in school and changed into upon arrival. That first day I tried to explain that I could not take my shoes off. They insisted I remove them. I remember crying bitterly. All day long I could imagine my legs bending crooked as I walked. A visit from my mother soon cleared this up and an exception was made for me. "As long as you wear rubbers, then wipe your shoes off well before coming into the class." However this was a bitter victory for this exception added more fuel to my 'differentness'.

Besides all my innate strangeness the fact that I was the only kid from the country in my class further isolated me. At noon there was an hour and a half break for children to walk home where a hot meal was awaiting them. The teachers also mostly went home to eat. Islanders called the noon meal 'dinner' since it usually was the biggest meal of the day. The idea of fast food eaten on the run had not yet come to the Island. I later learned that 'lunch' was little squares of sweets with small tuna, chicken salad or ham sandwiches usually served with tea in the afternoon or evening as part of another event.

For me 'dinner' was eating alone in my classroom. There was little supervision for country kids when the teachers went home to eat so we were confined to our classrooms and expected to keep out of trouble until the last half hour outdoor recess when the children began to return after eating. My brother had three or four other country kids in his class to keep him company but I was on my own.

Eating couldn't fill the whole hour so I fantasized the time away. Opening my tin lunch can I slowly and deliberately unwrapped my sandwich from its waxed paper. What have we got today? A nice ham and cheese and an extra jam sandwich. I poured the milk from the metal thermos with its glass lining into the cap which served as a cup. Next I munched on the yellow russet apple thinking about the cool red-soil cellar at home full of apples – apples that had been picked from our own orchard before our arrival and thoughtfully left for us. I imagined next spring sitting on a sloping branch of the apple tree in the center of the orchard hidden by the fragrant white and pink blossoms. And later in the autumn lounging and munching on the fresh juicy ripe fruit picked right off the branch overhead.

I glanced at the big clock up on the back wall. The long hand had to move all the way around before recess. It wasn't moving very fast. I had brought my paper dolls with me. We had numerous adventures together, dressed in different outfits appropriate for the occasion. I imagined many continuing dramas for them at home, at school, at church...

With permission I could read books borrowed from the reading library but I was not allowed to touch anything else in the classroom. As the endless hour continued I started to wander around the classroom looking but not touching. I stood for a long time in front of a poster which read, "When two vowels go walking the first one does all the talking." A round-bodied *a* and *i* walked hand in hand, *a* with a round smiley mouth and *i* silent and demure. The next poster was about spelling vowel sounds – "*i* before *e* except after *c*" it authoritatively stated.

That long hand was still crawling around. What else can I do to pass the time? The blackboard had been prepared with the afternoon meanings: a list of words and fill-in-the-blank sentences. I filled in all the blanks mentally. That was easy. Three pieces of attractive 'no-no-don't-touch' chalk - white, yellow and pink - laid on the small ledge along the bottom of the board. Above the blackboard were maps rolled up and tied with a cord. I knew that with one small tug Canada, or even the whole world with colour-coded countries, would unfurl in front of my eyes. Canada was such a big pink land, I remembered. Other countries were also pink and I had been told that all these pink countries proudly had the same Queen Elizabeth. I imagined the children in all these pink countries singing 'God Save the Queen' every morning in school as we did.

PEI is so small on the map yet it seems awfully big to me when we go for our Sunday drives. The world must be terrifically big! Alongside the board stood a yard stick. I knew that three of our foot rulers could be placed along the yard stick and I also wondered if my little 6-inch ruler which I carried in my pencil case would line up beside the yard stick six times. Let's find out...look at that! It's longer than six times because of the little extra piece at each end.

I looked curiously at the 'out-of-bounds' teacher's desk dominating the front of the room and facing all the children's desks standing in rows. Three neat piles of small sized Hilroy scribblers labeled Spelling, Composition or Arithmetic stood on the desk. On the back cover of these you could find handy spelling rules, examples of sentence punctuation or multiplication tables.

Big windows looking out unto the school yard lined one whole wall. Still no movement out there. Only one leaf still fluttering on the tree in its winter bareness. That reminds me of the Viking, Leif the Lucky. Leif! What a funny name for a man, but a good name for a leaf.

At long last I heard voices outside and saw teachers and children gathering for recess. It was so cold I hesitated to go out for noon recess while the others were coming back from dinner. This day I decided to go out. Recess was the only opportunity to play and meet others. Although we girls always wore skirts to school these were tucked into one-piece snow suits consisting of padded pants and jacket with a hood. A woolen cap, scarf and mittens completed this ensemble. On my feet were my lined overshoes with straps buckled tightly to keep the snow out. Despite this I was very cold just standing there outside while other children greeted each other and chased each other around keeping warm. No one seemed to even notice me standing there. Or perhaps they were too shy to approach this strange new person.

Finally the afternoon bell rings and we all troupe back into class. There stands the teacher with a face like a storm cloud. A hush falls over the chattering pupils. To our horror someone has scribbled all over the blackboard. Who could have done this dreadful deed? It was forbidden on pain of death to even touch a piece of chalk!

I hear my name being called to come forward. How could this have anything to do with me? All eyes turn to me as I stand in front of the blackboard. I hear the voice of the teacher as if from afar. She's accusing me of 'messing up' the blackboard. I must have done it, she tells me, since no one else is allowed in the classroom at noon. She commands me to wash the board, and then tells me to sit in the back corner of the classroom until I am ready to apologize.

Such a long afternoon, thinking and thinking "How can I apologize for something I didn't do?" My mind is racing so fast I see and hear nothing that happens until the bell rings for the end of the day. Everyone is leaving while I wait, still and silent.

"Well?" says Mrs. MacDonald. I wait, my head hanging.

"I will have to write a note to your father if you don't apologize."

Silence, as I stare at my toes.

"Well?" she repeats. "Are you sorry?"

"Yes." I whisper.

I was very sorry.

Salt of the Earth. *Author's note: As time went on I settled into Island life on the farm.*

One day, I was helping my mother make supper for the family. Macaroni and cheese! We were cooking on the old black wood stove. The fire was burning well and the water for macaroni was soon boiling. Without thinking I automatically spooned in some salt before dropping the macaroni noodles in. I scurried about setting the table for the five of us. A hesitant thought past through my mind. "Did I remember the salt?" So I shook a bit of salt in, just in case. Meanwhile my mother saw the noodles bubbling away in the water and thought, "I'm sure Blanche forgot the salt again." Not wanting to complain to me constantly about my forgetfulness she also sprinkled in some salt. As I was grating the cheese my inner voice started to nag me. I heard my mother's voice reminding me to 'be sure to add enough salt to the macaroni'. So I added a pinch more for good measure.

Supper was ready. My father, my two brothers, my mother and I filled steaming plates of macaroni and cheese – my brother's favourite and a favourite of mine too. But not this time! I took one heaping forkful and spit it out. I noticed everyone doing the same. Yuck! It was unbearably salty! No one could eat it that night. Not even my father whose cardinal rule was, "Whatever your mother cooks for supper, we eat it."

In one corner of the back yard which bordered on the pasture there was a place where leftovers, potato peelings and other food scraps were dumped and whichever farm animal who liked it was free to come to eat. The cow, the horses, the chickens, the dog, the barn cats - or even the wild animals, squirrels, mice, birds - all were welcome to enjoy. A kind of animal smorgasbord. I noticed the barn cat particularly enjoying the feast that night. It must have been the cheese – not a usual item on the buffet. I don't remember what we ate that night but I have a vague feeling of peanut butter and molasses on bread. The animals were bedded in the barn for the night and we were all snug upstairs in our beds dreaming about a hearty breakfast.

My early morning, pre-breakfast chore was to water the yearling calf in the barn. To do this I had to fill a bucket at the only source of water, the hand pump in the front yard, and carry it to the barn for the calf to drink. I was rather small for my age and I didn't have the strength to carry a full bucket of water. I found it easier to carry two half buckets. I was struggling with the stubborn latch at the barn door so I set the water buckets down in order to open the door.

Cats are known to hate water and avoid getting wet. But when I managed to open the door a black streak dashed out and jumped head first into the water. That was some thirsty cat!

My Special Place. *Author's note: Memories of my childhood return me to a sense of timelessness and freedom. No neighbours could be seen in any direction from the farm where I grew up on the Island. I was free to roam the farm without adult supervision. No one ever knew of my secret hiding place.*

VOICES

*I follow the lane
that runs across the pasture
entering the wooded hillside's
cool, dark enchantment.*

*Look, there! Flittering through dancing patches of sunlight,
A flash of fairies.
And there! Under an ancient, hollow tree,
Is that Peter Pan and his eternal troupe?*

*Shuffling though the long summer grass,
I find treasures of wild blueberries and strawberries.
While snacking on my way,
Grasshoppers spring in joyful welcome.*

*And then, through a secret gateway
Spruce branches swishing closed with a whisper,
Leaving no sign of entrance or exit,
I'm there!*

Blanche Moyaert: Becoming an Islander

My secret enclosure was an isolated island where the outside world no longer existed. The floor of this sanctuary had been covered with spruce needles which I had carefully swept to the bare ground. An aged grandfather of a tree had long ago fallen, gracing me with a ridge pole for the rough lean-to constructed from a discarded piece of canvas and unused wire fencing. I had hand carved the tent pegs myself. Cached inside a rusty metal tobacco tin with a snug fitting lid were my supplies – a multifunctional jackknife, a gardening spade, wooden safety matches, a small barbeque grate, a dual-purpose saucepan/drinking cup and other survival necessities. Towards the front of the lean-to and centered in the almost circular space, a ring of stones acted as a small fireplace. The friendly, long-dead ashes were a smoky reminder of onetime feasts and musings. Beside the fireplace sat a jumbo-sized soup tin for catching rainwater.

Lying on my back during the endless clear summer days, I could look through a grid of branches to the sky winking above. Closing my eyes I'd hear the birds fluttering and chattering to their neighbours. When I sat motionlessly other inhabitants might appear. A curious squirrel making a vacillating approach touches my fingers then scampers away. An inquisitive fox poking his nose around a tree stares before he turns away with one last friendly glance. When I sought sanctuary from a summer shower, I didn't mind sharing my shelter with the ant colony occupying my tree beam for they always put on an interesting spectacle.

Too soon the sun would leave my patch of sky. Sounds of voices, tractors and horses returning from the fields broke my solitude. Mama had told me to be sure to be home by supper-time!

A few years ago I had tried to find my secret place again. The farm house now had four or five close neighbours. The pasture was grown up with shrubs and the lane was hardly visible. When I passed through the woods, Peter Pan and the fairies were gone!

The well-developed trees now blocked a great deal of light and didn't allow for berry-covered, grassy places. The joyful grasshoppers had also moved on. I could not find the gateway to my secret place! Through time everything had become unrecognizable. I did not know which had altered the most –my special place or me.

VOICES

Nancy Perkins

I have always enjoyed reading and I once held five different library cards. I grew up and lived much of my life in New England. I began painting in 1948 and I was always attracted to the sea and marine landscapes.

My husband and I came to Prince Edward Island on one of our camping vacations and in 1984 my husband retired from teaching and we moved here to establish an inn which we remodeled from two barns. We were to operate the inn for sixteen years and some of my stories are based on my experiences.

As I see paintings form in my head, so I also see life around me become written stories. The Island is a very spiritual place to me and the colours of the sea and land nurture my creativity. I also enjoy gardening and quilt-making.

I am the founder of the annual Sea Glass Festival and am a volunteer at the Wood Islands Lighthouse. I am currently a member of Artisans on Main and show my paintings there and at the Dunes gallery and the Rossignol Winery has chosen some of my paintings to feature on their labels. I am working on illustrating a children's book by the author Terry Kerr to be published in November, 2014

I live in Montague in the winter and Little Sands in the summer.

VOICES

The Gosh Darn Plow

*Surveying the mailbox scene, or do
   mailboxes have feelings?
Here we are in many shapes,
   colours, designs, and names.
Here we are, all standing in a row.
   Smashed ones, banged ones,
Some standing on their head, all
   victims of a snow plow which
   left them all for dead.
Winter's hapless derelicts, parts
   flapping in the wind,
Contents shamefully exposed. Oh,
   it's such a sin!
The snow bank holds it sideways,
   there stands one.*

*New floor and door, but the battle has not been won.
All dressed up and raring to receive; a mailbox gets a new-earned reprieve.*

*The mailman comes and he laughs himself silly, pats us on our banged up
   head and says, "That one's sure a dilly!"*

*We should have a human wardrobe, like a real good sloppy and company best,
This would give the variety needed and we wouldn't be such a mess.
The humans could have a craft class
   'How to Find a Used Mailbox
   and Restore'.
They could study 'A Snow Plow's
   Attitude towards a Mailbox'
   and understand a whole lot
   more.*

*Halloween has come and gone and
   those who are still left standing,
Can only look forward to winter when
   the attacks are so demanding.*

*We love to warm our backsides, the
   summer sun so shining.*

Nancy Perkins: The Gosh Darn Plow

*Our spirits are rekindled in the absence of plows on roads so winding.
We hold the unchallenged position of comics true in all of PEI.
And the tourists grin and point to us, and we give a great big sigh.
My owner comes and reshapes my body, a tuck and a pull here and there.
It feels good, I can't tell you how good it really does, I declare!*

*Our dreaded time is far away now, a memory dim and battered.
The time has come to sing in the sun, to be singled out and to be so flattered.*

*So fix us up and love us, and go easy on the hammers and drills.
We will reward you with feelings of pride and hold back the terrible bills.*

*We stand here in the good and the worst of weather.
We never complain, but we do vow…that if we could aim our flag at our tormenter,
It would be the Achilles heel of that gosh darn plow!*

VOICES

The Ice Floe

In the spring on the Island the ice floes can become mountains of ice sometimes forming large bridge-like areas stuck to the shore. They are quite beautiful and very worthy of photo taking.

One day in late April my husband and I set out to do this. Although I was told not to do what I did, I did it anyway. I walked out on a very large piece of ice to take some photos. Everything went fine until there was the sound of a crack and the floe I was on broke in two.

It was amazing how one leg was on one side and the other leg on the other. I was doing an unintentional leg split. I did not want to fall into the icy water and although it was not deep, it would be most unpleasant to be wet and cold.

With my husband yelling "I told you so!" and calling me a fool among other things, I managed with every reserve of strength I had to pull the two pieces together. I was able to crawl over one piece and then off to land.

In telling the story later, I was told that the ice was 'rotten ice' and not to be trusted. I did get some nice pictures though, so I think it was worth it.

Nature Lovers

Bayberry Cliff Inn bed and breakfast in Little Sands, PEI, was well established as the place to stay when you wanted to be on a cliff and thirty feet from the edge.

"On the water?" prospective guests would ask.

"Of course, you could throw a ball over the cliff," I would answer.

This day however, the view from the edge offered the unexpected sight of two of our guests sunning themselves in the nude on our chaise lounges. I was hanging up the laundry on an upper deck when I observed our uninhibited guests. Another guest, a man from New York, was chatting with them. He acted like this was the most normal sight to see, nude people at a family B&B. I was rather concerned because these same two guests had asked earlier that morning about playing badminton.

They got up and strolled over to our stairs down to the shore. Our next door neighbor, several fields over, called and joked about Adam and Eve staying with us. We had a good laugh over this.

Their visit lasted three days and we held our breath the whole time. We did not want to appear stuffy and old fashioned so we said nothing. We never mentioned their non-attire to them and hoped they would use good judgment in walking around.

This visit stayed in our memory a long time. If that was their intention, they succeeded.

VOICES

The Blue Jar

Cleaning up the yard in the spring was always a chore. The raking and trimming should have been done in the fall, but when the weather turned cold, it was put on hold.

As I raked around the roots of some old bushes, I discovered a lot of bumps in the soil. Further inspection showed parts of dishes and old bottles. When I discovered a deep blue glass jar, I was ecstatic. I recognized it as a Vicks Vaporub container. This brought back memories of my childhood when I was sick in bed. My mother would rub Vicks on my chest to make me better with my bad cold. The hands rubbing it and its pungent aroma stay with me still.

Over the years, that Vicks jar has been in my medicine cabinet, but I cannot throw it out. Sometimes the empty jar holds pennies, sometimes flowers in the window. I move it from place to place but I cannot throw it out.

Many years ago, people did throw out their bottles. I know that the Vicks Company is one hundred years old. This makes me wonder how old my jar is and also about the people who used it and had no further use for it.

Now I walk on the shore and find pieces of blue glass all smooth and frosted because they have turned into *'sea glass'*. They have become a joy to anyone who sees them on the sand and I hurry to pick one up and hold it to the light.

That blue piece now rests against my throat and chest, part of a piece of jewellery. It swings back and forth, as I display it proudly. It has value again.

Island Blue

The Island has twenty-three shades of green;
I have never counted, so it remains to be seen.
What I do know, in my paintbox waiting for me,
Is cobalt blue for a deep blue sea.
Then there are French, Cerulean, and Prussian too;
These are my colours for the Island Blue.

From Original oil painting by Nancy Perkins

VOICES

The Astronaut Visit

"You didn't tell me you had an astronaut staying with you!"

These words were spoken to me by a friend in an early morning phone call to our bed and breakfast inn, Bayberry Cliff which we operated in Little Sands, PEI.

"Really, I didn't know we had one," I replied.

I did know something about astronauts, such as the landing on the moon. One staying at our place was outside my order of thinking. I then heard the story about how Colonel Chris Hadfield had gone to Orwell Corner the night before with his wife, Helena, and had entertained at the local Ceilidh. He sang and played his guitar. This was the same collapsible guitar he took into the spacecraft. The NASA program wants their astronauts to be well rounded. They are picked out of thousands of applicants and their other abilities help to keep their minds in good mental state.

'So, now I have one, what do I do about it?' I wondered. My husband Don said, "I knew he was military by the way he walked." My only clue was that Helena booked their three day stay from Texas, which I did not associate with the NASA program.

We had another guest who had a birthday that day. It was our custom to put a candle on a cupcake and sing Happy Birthday. With great casualness (although I was bursting with the news) I said, "We have another special guest this morning, Colonel Chris Hadfield and his family." The Colonel was very gracious and gave out autographed photos of himself in his space suit.

Then the big moment came when I invited him and his family to the Wood Islands lighthouse. I was part of a volunteer group, which, along with the Coast Guard was going to open up the closed-up structure that day to see inside for the first time in many years.

Since then the lighthouse has had three astronauts visit. Fifteen years later Colonel Hadfield is retired and the Wood Islands Lighthouse has had thousands of visitors from all over the world each year.

Nancy Perkins: The Astronaut Visit

VOICES

Booms in Little Sands

In 1984, we were building our Bayberry Cliff Inn as a B&B in Little Sands, Prince Edward Island. We were remodeling an old barn and were spending a lot of time outside. And then we began to hear strange sounds.

Very loud booms would occur over the open water.

The sleeping dogs would jump up and things would shake and rattle. This would go on every day and only in our area and sometimes in the nearby village of Wood Islands. A magazine, *Environment Canada* and other inquiring minds asked about it. No one had the answer. Much like the famous burning ship out on the Northumberland Strait, it was a mystery.

After *Environment Canada* became involved with papers to fill out about the time of day, wind conditions, weather and other data, nothing happened.

We never heard another boom. It remains unsolved.

Tom Rath

Written and oral communication play a major role in Tom Rath's life as an Islander. During his first two-year stint in 1979-81, he was commissioned by Tourism PEI to write twenty stories about the Island, and also authored the chapbook '*Souvenir of the Island*'.

During the years following his return to the Island in 1996 he has been recognized as the Island's Tourism Operator of the Year (2001) and the area Chamber of Commerce's Member of the Year (2005). This recognition was in part thanks to a 180-page website promoting his bed and breakfast, an annual thirty minute tourism radio program produced for broadcast at the NFL ferry terminal, and a 'Titanic Disaster' display produced and voiced at Cape Bear.

Tom is the author of an ongoing series of '*Donkey Oatie*' children's books, each one of which features illustrations by a different young Island artist. His other books include '*The KittenCat Adventures*', '*You're An Islander*' and '*Lady Catherine's Kitchen*'. He was a writer/editor of the lifestyle magazine *Island Living*, and has lectured on writing and public speaking, motivation and cooking. He is currently helping compile the forthcoming '*Heritage Kitchens of Kings United Pastoral Charge*' book. Other volunteer work includes mentoring of writing groups in Georgetown, Morell and Montague.

He and his wife and three fur-children (Moxi the dog, and cats Watson and Miss Kitty) live in Eastern Kings County, and can be reached at *tom.rath@yahoo.ca* or Facebook.

VOICES

Connections

In many ways, Islanders By Choice are the same as other Islanders. Fortunately, they are increasingly treated no differently, despite rumours to the contrary.

However, when someone from Eastern Prince Edward Island passes away, subsequent events make it more apparent there are still a few ways in which *Islanders by choice* differ from those born on the Island. My 17+ years here have equipped me with lots of background knowledge but not compared to that of Islanders who may have grown up in the same house as their grandparents. That's why IBC's like me are astounded and totally confused when somebody quickly rattles off phrases like, "Oh yes, he's a second cousin to my brother-in-law's first wife."

Let's start with the first announcements of his passing. I'm not talking about what appears eventually in the weekly Eastern Graphic or the daily Guardian's Obituaries/Funerals page. No. The latest news is shared at Tim Horton's at the old-men or young-ladies tables.

Here's where that difference first becomes notable. I know the deceased of course, thanks to daily interface. He was my neighbour, a service person, a member of my church or of Seniors College, the Rotary, the Montague Library Writers Guild or another of the many organizations that fill our spare time. But others around the table went to school with the deceased and therefore know him as a leaf on one of the many branches of a large family tree.

I'm always surprised at the viewing. To go through the receiving line and find myself expressing my condolences to a large group of other individuals I know, but learning only then that each one of them is a relative of the deceased.

Later, once all the formalities have been concluded, we all crowd downstairs at the church for a lunch of sandwiches, squares and hot beverages, to share the stories which bring closure but at the same time keep the memory of the deceased alive.

If I live in a large city for a few years my circle of relatives, friends, neighbours and business contacts eventually totals a hundred or so, one or two of whom may pass on over the course of five or ten years. This rare occasion means that I may feel awkward as to protocol and that any children in attendance will likely be a bit traumatized by the unusual event.

Here in Eastern Prince Island, where most people live within a circle of thousands, attending such farewells can be a weekly event. This makes farewells more a recognition and affirmation for adults and children alike that while death occurs regularly in our Island community, life itself goes on.

Unexpected Dinner Guest

I was serving supper to five guests at my Victorian farmhouse bed and breakfast. It was a special evening and the pressure was on. Why? Because one of the five was a travel writer doing research for the next edition of his popular travel guide and I knew everything would have to be perfect.

My table setting featured impressive antique china and cutlery. My appetizer brought forth murmurs of pleasure and empty plates, as did the entrée.

All I needed to make the meal a complete success was to serve my famous apple flan, a sure hit. I smiled confidently and perhaps a little smugly as I gathered up the main dish china and headed back to the kitchen to put the finishing touches on the dessert. Just seconds later, I whirled around in response to alarmed noises from my guests. Apparently as I was leaving the dining room in one direction a bat was fluttering into the dining room from another.

Perhaps it had come down the chimney and out from the fireplace. I never did find out. I did manage to encourage it back into the living room, then into the front hall and finally out the front door.

Yes, dessert was well-received although I don't recall the positive comments. What I will never forget, however, is the disturbingly amused expression on the face of the travel writer.

VOICES

Visitors are Surprised

Here in Eastern Prince Edward Island it surprises us to learn what surprises visitors. Sometimes it's a little thing to us, something to which we'd say, "Isn't it like this everywhere?"

On the other hand, particularly if we ourselves have done time in Toronto or New York, we smugly smile to ourselves and remind each other how fortunate we are to live where we do. Here are a few times when I've noticed that visitors are surprised:

When they learn how busy we keep ourselves after they leave at the end of summer. The Rotary Library here in Montague hosts over twenty activity groups including the writing group that published this and two previous compilations of stories, verse and essays. I can attend practical and lecture classes provided by Seniors College, Community School and private instructors, join support groups, service clubs, business organizations, age-specific activity groups such as 50+, and special-interest clubs such as bridge and gardening. Brenda and Edgar host well-planned Christmas, Easter and whenever potluck gatherings for one of our social groups and Ruth and Kenny host another one on Christmas Eve. Another group of our friends gather regularly for a themed potluck and we have our choice of similar events organized by area churches and community organizations. We go to ceilidhs, concerts, benefits, and other events in the area and occasionally in 'town' (Charlottetown).

When I tell them how local my food suppliers are. As an innkeeper in the tiny unincorporated community of Murray Harbour North I relied on neighbours David for my beef, Leon for my scallops, Glen for my lobster, John B. for my honey and John T. for my eggs and chicken. Assorted other neighbours brought me fresh produce. Barry used to show up at 8:30 with a flat (twelve boxes) of freshly-picked strawberries for my guests to sample. Now we live the same distance (fourteen miles or twenty-two kilometres) the other side of Montague and my lamb comes from George, fish from Raymond and eggs from Rae. I go to farmers markets in Cardigan, Morell and Montague to stock up on John D's freshly-baked breads, John and Susan's organic

Tom Rath: Visitors are Surprised

produce and everybody's preserves and baked (really) goods.

To see how different everything is from life in the big city. I used to set out lawn chairs on the lawn of my B&B and invite guests to grab an afghan and come out to look at the sky. I explained to one guest that that white thing up there was the Milky Way. I helped them recognize constellations, satellites and occasional comets. Guests were sometimes concerned at the prospect of driving in darkness, being more accustomed to the harsh glare of city lights than the relaxing glow of evening stars.

To realize that despite our small population, guests can worship at a variety of churches. Besides Catholic, Presbyterian, United, Baptist and other mainstream denominations, there are Jehovah's Witness, Church of Christ and numerous other active choices to welcome them.

In noticing the front door on many houses here in rural PEI. In many cases the front door is never used and that the steps, if they exist at all, lead out to the lawn itself or to a fully-enclosed deck. Instead, people go to the back door, which typically opens to an over-sized country kitchen. That's where residents and guests spend much of their time, not in the living room which is for more formal events. By the way, an evening of storytelling, music and family entertainment is the origin of the phrase 'kitchen party', which in turn is the origin of 'ceilidh'.

In also noticing those same lawns, be they a quarter acre or so in size, are kept so trimmed and attractive. It's not a law, it's more because everybody else's lawn is done nicely, too – a major demonstration of the pride of place that people have in living here. You'll see numerous signs directing you to our treasured attractions such as beaches, theatres and the above-mentioned farmers markets instead of billboards extolling the virtue of travelling elsewhere. Islanders do escape to Mexico or other southern destinations for a week or two as a reprieve from winter weather or venture to Alberta for bouts of more lucrative employment but they always come 'home' to Prince Edward Island.

VOICES

Don't 'Stop Playing With Your Food!"

At age six, I was the oldest of four children, raised by a returning WW II veteran and his frazzled 1950's housewife in a seven-hundred square foot wartime house in London, Ontario. We ate in the tiny kitchen because the dining room was rented out to a boarder. Dad had taught Mom how to cook, and occasionally took over, making us his French toast breakfast. We ate it all, basting the first few slices with ketchup, then a final one with jam for dessert.

We talked a lot between ourselves, as kids do, until a frustrated "Shut up and eat your face!" brought sudden silence followed by gales of laughter.

We learned about exotic foods such as chicken livers, and on one memorable occasion, even *cheval*.

My sister Pat took over the hosting of holiday family dinners in later years but each of us learned to keep exploring options, opportunities and oddities. I later became an innkeeper and developed ways to make even the trickiest meals look attractive and memorable.

At age seven my future wife Fran was also the oldest of four children raised in the heart of Montreal with English, French and Hungarian in her lineage. Her grandfather was the minister of the Hungarian United Church and her father was known by area butchershop owners as the man who was always seeking out organ meats to use in preparing such delicacies as liver dumplings.

It's a different world today and for many there is simply no time to spend over a hot stove. That's a shame, because here on Prince Edward Island we have a wealth of fresh seafood, meats, poultry and a wide choice of organic farmers eager to share their bounty with us. It has been said that if you enjoy what you do, you'll never work a day in your life. In my opinion that also applies here and now if you remember and haven't unlearned that important lesson from your childhood. You can find time for one of the most creative, fulfilling and fun hobbies right at home in your kitchen, playing with your food.

Winter Whirl

This past winter has featured a seemingly endless series of blizzards followed by one-day teasers to let my guard down, followed by more blizzards. I realize everyone has had their share but that doesn't make it any easier to smile in February. What does make my day however, is the way neighbours respond to my big-city-bred frustration with such events.

It was just two weeks ago that I drove gingerly down my driveway. The surface was quite clear as rain had melted much of the hard-packed snow accumulated during the latest downfall. I gave my trusty Versa the gentlest burst to help it up and over the relatively small snowbank left by the community snowplow.

It was when I turned the wheel that I realized just how slick the surface of Weatherby Road had become. The car did in fact turn out of the driveway to the right as expected but then it drifted diagonally across the two lanes, coming to a gentle stop with my left front fender nuzzled securely into the large snowbank on that side of the road.

I sat there for a moment or two, after trying unsuccessfully to free the car in either direction, then glanced through my rearview mirror as a second car came slowly pirouetting towards mine. Odd timing, as there are only two of us with Weatherby Road addresses.

Thanks to the mild grade of this unpaved road the slick surface caused by sheer ice and our mutual good fortune, her car's graceful 360-degree dance ended harmlessly across the road from my vehicle, some twenty feet further ahead.

"I was sure I was going to hit you," she said as we stood together, examining our mutual predicament.

Within minutes we were joined by passersby Raymond with a truck of ashes, and Terry with a truck of salt. Each hacked into the snowbanks with their shovels, tossed their preferred traction-treatment at the tires and had our respective vehicles freed in no time flat.

Once we arrived at the end of Weatherby Road, conditions were vastly improved and the day carried on, thanks to the spontaneous helpfulness of our Island neighbours.

Fur-Children

Is parenting one or more fur-children different in rural PEI than in the big city? My wife and I think so.

Our family (two adults, two cats and one dog) lives in a large house just outside the village of Bridgetown. Our lot size is about four acres of lawn and woods above the Boughton River. Considerably different from your situation, if you live in a suburban bungalow on a lot size 50x50, or in an apartment downtown. The major difference? Danger.

You probably don't worry a lot about coyotes and bald eagles, both of which share our jurisdiction. I was somewhat startled a few years ago to read a thought-provoking piece of trivia. The percentage of animals living in the wild that die a violent death isn't the 20 to 30% I automatically guessed but more like 100%. Coyotes and bald eagles are always on the alert and we don't like the thought of feeding such expensive meat to feral diners. Thus, our dog Moxi enjoys carefully supervised nature calls and exercise walks so that she won't be quite as exposed. Our cats, Watson and Miss Kitty, are strictly housebound and use their litter box in the basement.

Another danger for Moxi is that tempting river that runs alongside our house. It would take only a quick run down the riverbank and she could be slowly swimming in summer or clambering on fragile ice in winter.

Admittedly, your pets face a lot more traffic. However, that means they are more aware of it. Trucks, cars, ATVs. Any one of them can be an intriguing and fast-moving novelty on the back roads.

So, is parenting fur-children different here? Certainly, because of the danger element. But on the other hand, it can be just as satisfying!

Tom Schultz

About thirteen years ago while a professor at Purdue University in Indiana Tom was drawn, with his wife, to PEI on vacation. A few years later he retired so they could spend their time fully at their house in Wood Islands.

He began self-publishing with a technical book and subsequently produced *'Prince Edward Island; Seen From Away'*—a book about his early experiences and impressions of PEI. He has been a member of the Montague Library Writers Guild from its beginning and has watched with amazement its growth and persistence. Since then he has published numerous books for local writers including the previous three editions of the Montague Library Writers Guild and at least ten other books written individually by members of the guild. He has two ongoing writing projects, a book about sailing and a book about Scripture study. In following the newer trends he has developed four eBooks and maintains five web blog sites:
www.woodislandsprints.com,
www.revisitingscripture.com,
www.candthe8051.com,
www.woodislandssailing.com
www.brooksidepei.ca.

In addition to writing and publishing, he is active in photography, teaching several courses for Seniors College as well as producing photo-products supplied to gift shops. He may be contacted at schultz@pei.sympatico.ca

Winter Night Drive Home

Come with us in imagination as we drive home from Charlottetown on a winter evening. Nine in the evening is now intensely dark. Once over the Hillsborough Bridge the yellow streetlights are few and far between. The lightly falling snow does not overcome the heavily salted road...at least as far as Sobeys. We shared the bridge with ten or fifteen cars, but most of them turn off to driveways and small subdivisions as we go along. By the time we are at the curve by the Irving station, only three or four cars are still with us. There is an annoyingly cautious car ahead, so we speculate as to whether it will take the left turn to Montague.

Marking that junction is Buster's gas station with its lit-up, tattered flag, an indicator of the wind speed and direction. Will there be drifting snow ahead? Surrounded by open fields, the wind arrives unhindered. The flag pole has a permanent bend that seems to exaggerates wind speed.

We go to the right straight under the sign for Wood Islands and the ferry. Of course, the ferry stopped running well before Christmas and we know the terminal is only a deserted collection of yellow lights at this time of year. The road shifts to being sanded rather than salted. When we reach Orwell Cove, the one or two vehicles that have continued with us either stay on the Trans-Canada toward Cooper's store or turn left toward Montague. Cars taking the quick left-and-right onto Selkirk road are rare, and if there are any they turn off by Iona.

Alone on the Road. From here, the winter road is our own and I drive down the centre to avoid any drop-off on the shoulder or encroaching drifts, either of which could pull the car off the road. My theory is that in the centre if I lost control on a patch of ice, I'd have more room to slide before hitting something on either side. I go a bit slower since there is no one behind and no appointments waiting at home. A couple of inches of light snow have accumulated since the plough last went through, leaving us to make virgin tracks. Where open fields are to the west this snow has already been converted to four to six inch drifts across the road. If we were to get stuck or break down along here, it would be a long walk for help.

We have seen no approaching headlights! At night, even over the top of a hill, light would give advance warning to move over for approaching traffic. On particularly bad nights, we go around on the Trans-Canada Highway in hopes of somewhat better road conditions, but even then, after the Belfast school, road conditions deteriorate quickly.

Regardless of the way we choose, a few houses are still lit up without curtains pulled, exposing their interiors to plain view. It is as though we are in their living rooms. The light from the TV screen has a bluish cast while the lamps are a warm yellow. With binoculars, I suspect I could identify the chosen TV program and even which pictures are on the walls! By Island custom, only privacy-seeking city folks use heavy curtains or shades to block out the outside world, or to save on heat. Perhaps this is symbolic of the security and safety Island communities have always known. Since there are almost never any humans out there in the country, why close the blinds?

Snug at Home. Arriving home, if you are still with us in imagination, push the automatic-door-opener button and we drive directly into our attached garage. Traditionally garages were detached, so Islanders are used to walking through the cold, or rain, to get into the house. Immediately on getting inside, someone has to go out to fetch more logs for the wood stove, a never-ending winter task. Every few hours, even in the middle of the night, someone has to bring in wood from the attached woodshed. Compared to heating with oil, wood saves several thousand dollars a year. As I have aged I find I normally wake up every few hours, so it is easy to keep the fire stoked. Freed from the tyranny of the morning alarm by retirement, I revel in choosing to extend the middle-of-the-night interlude to read or surf TV channels for a late-night movie…because I can!

Winter Night Sounds

"…*outside were free hills and wide, open fields where you could run wherever you liked, none daring to make you afraid, spruce barrens and shadowy sand-dunes, instead of an iron fence and locked gates. And how quiet it all was…no honking, no glaring lights. Jane had pushed the window open and the scent of fern came in. Also a strange, soft far-away sound…the moaning call of the sea. The night seemed to be filled with it.*"[1]

Before coming to Prince Edward Island I would have said this is artistic exaggeration at work. Wrong! Some eighty years after those words were first written the description still perfectly describes a rural Island night.

Living Room Sounds. Since all our heat comes from a central, main-floor wood stove, the house is very quiet. There is no *click* of a thermostat, no *whoosh* of an oil burner starting, and no sound of a fan kicking in. The loudest night time sound comes when the refrigerator is running. Sometimes I hear a small *hum* from the CFL bulbs that have been replacing incandescent lighting. Oh yes, there is the *ticking* of the battery-powered clocks. They are a boon in areas such as ours with power outages. It is amazing how loud a ticking clock

---

1. L. M. Montgomery; *Jane of Lantern Hill*; 1936, McClelland & Stewart, Ltd, Toronto p112-113 (near end of chapter 17)

can sound at night! By the way, a *tide* clock can give you an indication of the high/low times at the shore based on the twenty-nine-day cycle of the moon. It is very clever, since the manufacturer merely adds a different crystal to the mechanism, changing the basic time interval, and puts on a different face. Sitting up in the quiet of the night, I can hear how the slight difference in the 'tick interval' shifts the two clocks in and out of sync about twice a minute.

Bedroom Sounds. All of that sound is far away... past a door, down the stairs, and around several corners. In the bedroom, with the windows slightly open there is no shortage of fresh air, except when a light breeze out of just the wrong direction lets wood smoke drift down the roof and in at a window. Since my spouse prefers a cool bedroom, I have taken to an electric blanket. Nothing is as snug as being in a freezing bedroom under several layers of covers, supplemented with an electric blanket as the inner layer!

Lying in bed, the quiet is intense. Summer will bring sounds of insects, peepers, and bullfrogs, mosquitoes beating on the screens and passing cars each time the ferry comes in. But for now, winter has stilled all that. Even with my declining hearing, I can hear my pulse beating in my ears. My mind plays tricks in the intense quiet. Some years ago I thought I was hearing music with a pronounced beat but I could never track down the offender. When I went outside to identify the direction, there was nothing. It must have been literally 'in my head'. If I could have captured such imagined melodies, I might have been a songwriter!

Outside Sounds. Gentle falling snow deadens sound but on a cold, still night you might hear a door close miles away. In our neck of the woods that would be about all the outside *human* activity to be heard. About the only *animal* sounds on a winter night come from the yipping of a coyote pack, perhaps on the trail of a rabbit. They sound much too close even when they may be a mile away. On very stormy nights, I may hear the sound of snow or sleet scouring across the window glass or the sound of the wind in the nearby spruce trees.

Though we live almost a mile back from the Northumberland Strait, when the wind is out of the south, especially on those stormy nights, we hear the sound of waves breaking on the shore. I imagine those waves having personality, attacking and trying to eat away the banks. Even though the shore cliffs by us are easily twenty feet high, a few feet of shore erodes away every year. In the spring, you can see spruce trees that have given up the fight, having tipped and slid down the bank to the breakers. By the way, if you decide to buy shorefront property, the government continues to tax you on the original area of the plot even when twenty to thirty feet of it may have gone over to the ocean!

One of Wood Islands' strangest night sounds is man-made. Sometime before 1890, the Coast Guard positioned a 'whistle' buoy several miles off shore to mark Indian Rocks which is a shallow stretch that comes out several miles and could be a threat to shipping. Locals call it 'the groaner' and when the wind is out of the southwest the sound easily carries the several miles to our bedroom. In the summer I have sailed out to see it and found it is a very large round buoy perhaps six feet in diameter. I understand it is chained to the bottom beyond the shallows at about thirty feet of depth and the sound is generated entirely by wave action. As a wave passes part of the buoy drops causing a bellows to take in air. As the next wave rises the lifting of the buoy drives the air out, making the low-pitched 'groaning' sound. Miles away lying snug in bed at night, as I hear each groan I can visualize a wave passing by out on the freezing water and pray there is no one in danger out on the water on such a cold night.

City folks may miss their traffic noise and all-night entertainments but I have come to love the quieter, slower pace. It is so snug to be safely at home in bed!

Island Funerals

This is adapted from my book, Prince Edward Island: Seen "From Away" *published in 2007.*

I am not an authority on funeral practices in general nor Island funerals in particular but I have found it interesting to see how much they are a part of local culture.

Returning Home. In some respects I imagine PEI is the Canadian equivalent of Florida in the US. It too is an area with a higher-than-average proportion of retirees who have come to end their days. In the case of Canada, this move is not probably for the warm climate, but rather to return to family and roots. Since there are relatively few well-paying, full-time jobs, on the Island many young folks must go off-island to find meaningful work in their area of training. For aspiring graduates Alberta, Toronto and Boston seem to be the places of opportunity and the 'brain drain' is significant. However, even though these young people move away, their large extended families serve as anchors to the Island. As they approach retirement they start to think of returning to their roots. They may have inherited the family homestead or just have a yearning to return to the quieter pace of life. So many young working people are elsewhere and older retired folks are back living on the Island, creating this higher proportion of the elderly.

The Island is a highly inter-related culture with large families. In fact, I have frequently overheard two elderly folks trying to determine the vital question of who exactly is an individual under discussion. The conversation might beguin, "Who is the John Mackenzie recently in the news for drunk driving?" This question is only answered when John's lineage back for at least two generations is established along with the locations of these progenitors. "Oh, he is a nephew of the Fred Mackenzie who lived on the Peter's Road in the 1940's."

Obituaries. With proportionally more old people you have proportionally more people dying. Just reading the obituaries gives me a sense of the number of elderly who end their days on the Island. I expect this drives the sales of newspapers because we are often surprised to later learn after the fact that someone died several months ago. We do not do a very good job of connecting with the local culture.

A significant portion of local radio news programs involves reading obituaries. It drives me up the wall in this nominally Christian province to hear the standard line that the deceased person is 'resting comfortably' (or is it 'peacefully'?) at such and such funeral home. Even a Christian in name only should take offense at that! The clarion call of the Christian faith is that at death the soul/spirit is not in or around the body! Their spirit has gone to be with the Saviour and the mortal body is now just a leftover shell! This mortal shall put on immortality, and the body returns to the dust. No one is out back 'resting' in the funeral home.

Viewing. Local culture sees a steady flow of evening visitors as evidence the deceased was well known and liked. A light attendance would say the opposite, I suppose. I dislike putting those closest to the deceased through the strain of a long extended calling period but tradition expects it. Even if the one closest to the deceased may not be able to endure the lengthy time, on the Island there is usually an extended group of relatives who step in to help receive condolences and reminisce. It can be an opportunity to celebrate a life as well as helping in the grieving process. Usually a picture of the individual is on display regardless of whether or not the casket is open. I suppose this is where the idea of 'resting' came to be associated with the body. The number of callers is something to boast about later. In my experience visitation is unlike a wake in that there is no food or drink provided. Perhaps the most public aspect of visitation is the long rows of cars that spill out along the street for overflow parking. It is a long walk along the highway to and from the parked car.

Funerals. Many funerals are early in the afternoon. They may draw those who did not attend the visitation or vice versa. Most funerals these days take place in the funeral home chapel although some are still held in churches. In most respects I suppose they are like funeral services across the US and Canada. The front seating is reserved for the relatives and there is a distinct order to their seating with immediate family toward the front and more distant relations further back. Someone delivers a eulogy and one or two others may reminisce about aspects of the deceased's life and good points. There may be the singing of favorite hymns and a brief sermon from the minister. Coming from a strong Christian tradition, I find it particularly upsetting when the minister has to resort to generalities because he has no idea of the spiritual state of the individual and had no personal acquaintance. Many grieving families still want a minister even despite no involvement with the church otherwise.

VOICES

To the Cemetery. There are many small, scattered cemeteries and relatively few funeral homes on the Island so, except in the deep of winter, the funeral service usually concludes with a long motor procession to the burial site. As the procession passes, most oncoming cars pull over in respect for the dead. Unfortunately since Canada has mandated that headlights always come on automatically even in the daytime it can be tricky to recognize an approaching funeral procession. I still vividly remember one particular day when I was coming back from town. There seemed to be a steady flow of traffic but I found a gap and pulled in. Once in line it seemed all the cars were going very slow. As I impatiently passed car after car wondering if *everyone* on the island drove excessively slow I got a glimpse of the hearse up ahead. How embarrassing! Of course I was driving my sporty convertible, giving a bad name to all of us from away. Funeral homes should supply little magnetic flags to put on each car so we foreigners can identify the procession.

Interment. The brief service at the graveside is an extension of the earlier funeral service. I have usually not taken the time to participate in them. I recall discovering that Billy Martin, a local character whose mowing business included the Wood Islands cemetery also dug graves. He had done so for decades and had done it all by hand! I asked him why by hand and his answer related to access for equipment in and around the other graves as well as tradition. I also learned that 'six feet under' is not literally true and the deepest burial might be six feet at the *bottom* of the casket, but could well be less. Anyway, after the interment there may be an invitation to stop by the house for refreshments. I suspect that is where the refreshments of a traditional wake may come in. It also makes a much more personal setting to celebrate the life of the individual, surrounded by the people that knew them best.

Donna Singleton

Donna has always loved writing, drawing, craftwork and people. Her writing has always been an escape from whatever trials were set before her.

Fiction was never really her thing. She enjoys real life stories like this little one from her old school days, an endearing recollection of how she and her family remember with fondness the dear old war veteran that became a part of her family many years ago.

Donna has entered many pieces in *The Eastern Graphic* over the years, be it holidays or just her opinion. She says, "Writing is my way of expressing myself, and my release from stress. I am in my own little world when I write, I just love it."

She aims someday to publish her own life story in hopes it will benefit others.

Born and raised on the Island she grew up in Belfast and married in her teens. Donna made her home in Murray River, PEI, with her husband Ronnie. She now has five grown children who are always welcome home.

VOICES

February 14th 1967

Tomorrow would be Valentine's Day in our one-room school in the community of Belfast, PEI. I was in Grade Seven.

Back then, school was similar to now but everything was not as commercialized. We had no computers or any sort of electronics. Maybe a transistor radio if we were lucky. As an Islander I knew we were not wealthy but was very appreciative of what we had. I guess I just never really noticed that we were not all the same, or just took it for granted. So on special occasions such as this one particular Valentine's Day at our school, I was really looking forward to heading off to school.

Mom was making my favorite scotch cookies. Each cookie was cut in the shape of a heart. I sat there drooling, knowing they were so good. Mom said "Now Donna, these are going to cool. I will ice them in the morning before you go, ok?"

"Ok Mom, can't I have just one now, before bed?" I begged, knowing she'd give in and chase me off to bed with my still warm delight.

"Take one and git. You're worse than your Dad. Now off to bed

Donna Singleton: February 14th 1967

with you."

My room was actually the attic part of the house. My heat source was the stovepipe that ran up through the ceiling, along the floor and up through the roof. It was great for drying things or warming up some blankets on a cold winter's night. The walls were the boards that covered the roof, which were pretty drafty. I remember awakening to a tiny snowdrift on my pillow and my long red hair frozen to it. Obviously it wasn't insulated so decorating the room with whatever I could find for the walls was very inventive. I made wall covering out of pieces of cardboard and drew pictures on them.

It was fun making curtains for the little window that overlooked the porch and Uncle Robert's wee house. I made them from a grand old skirt of Mom's or some old hand-me-down. Dear little Aunt Frances from Scotland always called their home 'our wee house'. She was a feisty little redhead who really kept Uncle Robert and Cousin Bobby in line. I so missed skipping across the field to visit Aunt Frances. She passed away to cancer as far as I know. She loved to give me gifts, which were very precious to me, such as a handmade little kangaroo, solid red on one side and red and black plaid on the other half. I adored it and took it home to try my hand at making one, perhaps for my little sister. There were many other treasures from Aunt Frances, such as a beautiful white and gold lace covered photo album with a music box on the side, which played 'I Love You Truly'. Then a gold set of clip-on earrings with rectangular green emeralds. Real or not they were priceless to a little girl from Belfast, PEI. I still have my earrings, with a little story of their own of how they disappeared and then returned to me.

I was content in my little attic room sewing doll clothes for my sisters and for my Suzie doll. My teacher (Mrs. Ross) gave her to me for Christmas in Grade One. Suzie is still with us to this day. She has always been precious to me, as was Mrs. Ross. This Christmas Suzie turned fifty-three years old and has lived with my twenty-three year-old granddaughter Alyssa since her first birthday.

Now back I go to February 14th, 1967...

The morning couldn't come quickly enough, I thought. Mom was up early and was almost done creating her little masterpieces. I watched eagerly as she squeezed the white icing into cupid arrows. Then the red frosting Out flowed little red hearts until each cookie looked like a little painting. I felt ever so special as I watched Mom place each cookie on her favorite rose plate.

"They're perfect Mom! I can't wait to bring them to school. Bye Mom, love you, Happy Valentine's Day," I shouted, throwing my Mom some Valentine kisses.

"Thank you dear, now get going. Cecil will be waiting." Mom said as she watched me run out the lane. Off I went proudly, my cookies displayed on Mom's pretty rose plate.

Farmer Cecil just lived a short distance from our place. I loved his animals and the fresh milk and eggs we always got from him but disliked the farm smells at the same time. Johnny and Charles were his boys. I really didn't mind getting a drive to school with them in Farmer Cecil's old truck. I often protested though that they should buy a new, and not so smelly car to drive us to school.

The sun glistening on the snow in the ditches dissolving into trickling streams always fascinated me that time of year. I was thinking to myself, "Maybe spring will come early this year, I sure hope so." Farmer Cecil's mailbox was still in the ditch. "That plowman should be more careful," I thought, annoyed. The morning was alive with the sounds of the farm as I walked up the lane. Then, hearing two ear-bursting backfires, I knew I had to hurry. Farmer Cecil's old black truck was running. His old floppy hat always darkened the rear window of his stinky old truck. I could hear the cows mooing in the barn.

"They must need milking," I thought.

Chickens were clucking. They must have some fresh eggs to be gathered.

"They'll just have to wait till Farmer Cecil drives us to school," I said to myself.

My green backpack was slipping off my shoulders as I hurried

Donna Singleton: February 14th 1967

up the lane. Everyone wanted one of these bags. My Mom bought it for me from the war surplus store. These bags used to belong to the soldiers. I peeked under the wax paper to see if my cookies were safe.

"Good," I sighed "they're ok,".

Just then Johnny and his brother Charles flung open the wooden screen door on their old white farmhouse and charged out swinging green army backpacks as well. Johnny yelled. "Want to ride on the back with us Donna? It's nice out!"

"I guess so. I have to be careful because my Mom made the prettiest Valentine cookies. They're on her best plate!" I beamed, grinning from ear to ear.

"Ok Donna," Johnny said, "we can still walk home after school if it's still sunny out, right?" Charles helped me up onto the back of the old stinky truck. I just nodded in agreement as Johnny spread the old army blanket out for us and off we went.

As we walked into the school I thought the table looked like we were about to dine with royalty. It was all draped with a fine white tablecloth covered with elegant dishes and rich food.

"Mrs. Ross, will you please put these on the table for me? There's a special Valentine cookie for everyone," I said still feeling very proud.

"Thank you, Donna. Be seated children. Roll call," she called out, pointing to us to be seated. "Well I'm pleased everyone is here today. Please stand for 'O Canada'."

Mrs. Ross was always such an especially nice teacher. We had no reason to misbehave, I thought, as she said, "Thank you. Now let's exchange our Valentines. We'll play musical chairs before we have our treats."

Mom had helped me make and colour my cards and I always considered our cards as special on any occasion. A little brown bear holding a red heart was for Mrs. Ross. As she opened it she gave me a nice smile and said thank you.

The two new Grade Eight bad boys looked at their cards, whispered something, but they hadn't given me a card. I was embarrassed and saddened, thinking my cards should have impressed them. Then Mrs. Ross said, "Come children, let's enjoy these lovely

treats." Well now, I thought, the boys will surely be impressed once they have one of Mom's special cookies.

Kids can be mean at any age and back then was no different from today. As in any school, there always seems to be three sets of social groups, the well-to-do, the middle class, and the lower class. I guess I was in the last group that day and many other days besides this one but I always brushed it off or just fought when provoked.

As the treats were handed out, I was eagerly awaiting the 'ooohs' and 'ahhs' that would confirm how delicious my cookies were. Some were gracious but then the rude gestures began and the comments like, "I am not touching them! They are MacLeans cookies. Yuck!"

The teacher scolded them but I was overcome with embarrassment and the shame that they had made me feel. All I wanted was to go home so Mrs. Ross excused us and told Johnny and Charles to walk home with me. The boys were good friends to me, more so then any of the girls. Guess maybe I was just like one of them. But this time, this really hurt, I was so disappointed and so embarrassed and bewildered at the same time. Why they acted as if I was some sort of poison was beyond my understanding.

Despite my thinking no one would ever misbehave with a wonderful teacher like Mrs. Ross, I was wrong.

There was lots of misbehaving that took place before the teacher arrived in the morning or at recess or dinner time. Once, the new boys from Iona decided to do some experiments with the stuff in the little corner set aside for science. Before the teacher arrived, they dumped a bunch of vials of chemicals or something in the big old stove that heated the school. The stove was already lit that morning by the janitor, I presume. Just as Teacher arrived there was

Donna Singleton: February 14th 1967

this loud bang as the covers of the stove flew off, nearly hitting the ceiling. Smoke and soot was flying everywhere. Needless to say the boys were in big trouble. I don't remember what their punishment was but those bad boys from away with their shiny black hair were so cute. I know the other girls in school liked them too but our admiration didn't seem to make much of an impression on those boys.

There was another young boy with sandy blond hair whose name was Allison I thought was so nice. He was either too shy to talk to me or he didn't like girls yet at the time. The bad boys must have known this for one day they ganged up on Allison and me. They herded us into the boy's bathroom in the porch part of the school and locked us in. He never said much more than for them to let him out and never said a word to me. He was such a handsome young man and I always remember Allison as a gentleman.

Many of my classmates have passed away or have lost contact with me but I wonder sometimes what they are or would be like now. In my early Grades I was always a bit of a tomboy in school and the older kids would always be pushing me to fight with the boys and sometimes the girls as well. For instance, one day they had us use the outdoor pump stand as a boxing ring. I fought that day because they had called me a nasty name. At the time, I didn't know what it meant. I suppose because I wore black leotards might have had something to do with it. But I usually won the scrap they arranged for me.

Eventually my title wore off and I studied hard and always loved to learn. I could never permit myself to fail in anything. I would be so disappointed in myself if my grades were not up to my standards. I was to experience many little disappointments, along with some proud moments of achievement.

We all go through the hurt of those first crushes on a classmate that doesn't seem to notice you and for me it was all part of the highs and lows of growing up on PEI.

VOICES

Russell (A Good Old Boy)

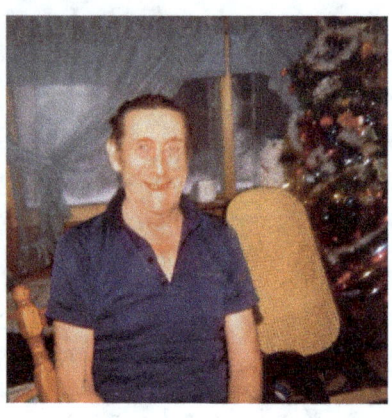

From the day Russell, sixty-year-old war veteran, asked if he could board with our family he became family. He was tired and needed someone to take care of him. He had been living in the old homestead at the edge of our community, Murray River, with his brothers Forest and Lester. The home was run down and the three men tried their best but weren't able to fend for themselves. Forest, the oldest of the brothers had just passed away. The poor man was attempting to light a fire in an old camper they had with lamp gas and it blew up He was burned to death. Very tragic. So when Russell humbly asked if he could stay with us we said, "Yes."

He was a special man. His appearance reminded me of someone you'd see sitting on a park bench feeding the pigeons. His light blue dress shirt with sleeves rolled up to his elbows, his sleeveless v-neck wool pullover vest, his favorite navy blue dress pants held up by suspenders, right down to his brown suede loafers curled to the shape of his once slender feet made Russell, Russell. His left leg was always stretched out as he sat, due to a war wound. His wooden cane always rested next to him. His favorite place was sitting at the table playing Solitaire, sipping tea, waiting for one us to have a game of Rummy with him. War leaves many scars on people. Not just physical but emotional as well and I believe he was left with many scars. I wondered what Russell's life would have been like had he been given a different path. Would he have married, had children, chosen a career he wanted to pursue and lived the life he may have dreamed of? I imagined the life that he could have had, if he had not joined the army and fought for his country.

My children grew up knowing Russell as their big brother, grandfather, best friend, card partner, a shoulder to cry on when needed, or someone who would just listen to them. Russell was whoever you needed him to be. But what did he need us to be? I like to believe we were the family he needed. I hope we were.

All five of our children have memories of time shared with good old Russell. Ask any of them what they remember:

My now forty-year-old daughter Kelly would likely say, "Russ liked that old Kelly's wine while we had a good old game of Rummy." Kelly shared many thoughts and problems during her younger teen years with Russ. Russ passed away on Kelly's wedding anniversary July 25th which is also my grandson Cody's birthday, July 25, 1999. Faithfully every year Kelly visits his grave and lays flowers and an angel for our Russell. In this way, for Kelly it's an honour to honour Russ, as he had chosen her day to remember him.

Tracy was a few months old when Russell came to our home. She once asked, "Mommy is Russ my brother?" This made sense to her, seeing he had always been there regardless that he was nearly three times Mommy's age. Tracy is thirty-seven now and dearly misses her card buddy. Many nights you'd see Russ and Tracy sitting at the kitchen table playing Rummy. She liked making Russ a good old cup of tea, then playing cards 'till they could stay awake no longer. She tells me she still dreams of Russ and believes he watches over her and protects her from harm.

My baby girl Veronica, now thirty-five, adored Russell. My little monkey girl, always with a banana in her mouth, making faces with that mischievous gleam in her eye had a way of making Russell laugh even when he seemed down. She liked to tag along with her uncle and his girlfriend when they'd take Russ for a trip on the ferry-

boat. They'd visit an old friend of Russell's, go to restaurants, take pictures, do a little souvenir shopping and head home. Veronica always had a fear of war and I think Russ used to ease her fears. There were times when Rucka (her nickname) would cry because something scary on the news about war had frightened her. All it took was, "Rucka, how about a game? Is there any tea in that pot? Come on girl. Best outta three's the winner."

That mischievous little smile and the gleam in those dark brown eyes came back as she climbed up in her place at the table yelling, "Mommy, Russ needs tea, we're playing *best outta three!*"

The children could always depend on Russ to talk to when they couldn't sleep. A good old game of cards could always calm their fears. They believed they were looking after *him*, getting his tea and keeping him company. Russell enjoyed nothing more than fish and potatoes. Fresh, salted or canned fish. It didn't matter and just like Popeye he loved spinach. Of all the children, Veronica was the only one that shared his love of fish.

My oldest boy Ron, now thirty-two, dearly loved our Russell as well. Like the others, he played cards with Russ, watched television, drew pictures and listened to Russell's war stories when he felt like telling them. Video games became the thing when Ron turned six and we gave him the new Nintendo. Russell would sit there watching him play and cheering him on as he played. As Ron got older his talks turned to comfort from Russ with his teen year problems.

Finally my baby boy Travis who is now over six feet tall and twenty-two years old, remembers Russell as his friend who would play Dinky cars with him anytime, taught him to play cards and always encouraged him to keep drawing as he had with Ron. His encouragement may have contributed to the artistic talent they have today. As with Ron, Russ patiently watched as Travis played his favorite video game. On Travis's sixth birthday Russ asked Trevor (how he said Travis) what he would like for his birthday. Russ was in the hospital at this time and this was in March of 1999. Travis told him he would like a new red controller for his Nintendo. Russell said, "Order him one, Donna." So I did. On his birthday Travis was so happy not only because he got his red controller but because this was the first gift Russell had ever given him, which made it beyond special. He kept that controller for years and it is most likely still in amongst all the systems collected here over the years.

I recall one day Travis was gazing out the window a few months after Russell had left us. He was thinking about Russell and this is what he said, "Mommy, look, do you see that cloud?"

I replied, "Yes sweetie, why?"

"Do you think Russ is up there picking corn for me?"

"I hope so Travis, Russ knows you love corn. I think someday you'll pick corn together up in the clouds sweetheart, ok?"

He thought about it for a moment, and said. "Is Russ going to wait for me up there Mommy?"

"Sure he will, but Russ wants you to keep busy drawing and grow up and do all the good things he told you that you could do. But that's far, far away. Russ doesn't want you to forget all the fun times you had with him and he'll see you later, ok?"

"Ok Mommy, I miss Russ."

"I know you do sweetheart, we all do. Remember Russ's watching over us up there in the clouds with God when you need him, ok?"

"Ok Mommy." That seemed to satisfy him, and he went back to

studying that cloud that he believed was where Russell and God were waiting for him.

Tears still fill my eyes when I think of the way my children remember Russell. I know he hears me when I say, "We miss you, and love you. God bless you Russell."

Russell Edward Hayter joined the army in 1943 and was a Private in the PEI Highlanders C.A. He was born September 5, 1918 and died July 25, 1999. Russell was dearly loved by the Singleton family whom he lived with in Murray River for many years.

Love always,
Mr & Mrs Ronnie Singleton

Kim Smith

Kim and her husband arrived on PEI in May 2008. They packed all their belongings in their semi, tossed in their three unsuspecting cats and went on to experience an incredible journey on the drive from Vancouver Island to Prince Edward Island, over-nighting in truck stops all the way.

Kim wrote as a teenager then stopped and thought she would never write again. However the move to PEI opened the floodgates of her creativity and despite her penchant for procrastination she has produced a fair number of stories and essays over the past few years. She has several articles on writing published in an online women's site, two articles published in *Countryside Magazine,* and has been awarded second and fourth places respectively in PEI and Nova Scotia literary competitions.

Other pursuits include reading, baking, collecting eggs from her own chickens and keeping her husband fed as he works on the house. You can read her blog at *www.peihome.wordpress.com*

VOICES

PEI Has Only Three Seasons

As my husband is so fond of jokingly saying, "PEI has only three seasons. Summer, Fall and Winter."

There is no spring on PEI. Sure, March 21st rolls around and it's officially spring in other parts of the world, but not here.

Spring on PEI is just an extension of winter. You may as well just call it Winter, Part Two.

So PEI really does have four seasons. Summer, Fall, Winter Part One and Winter Part Two.

Winter holds fast in January and February. Quite dreadful, really. Meanwhile, on Vancouver Island, early rhodendrons are in bloom along with snowdrops and crocuses. Sure they get some minus temperatures and a bit of snow, but really? It's like comparing David and Goliath! And please note, Anna's hummingbirds stay all year around on Vancouver Island. I've no idea what they eat, but what does that tell you, eh?

March, though my heart soars at the very fact that it IS indeed March, is still pretty much still winter. Sure the temperatures inch up a few degrees. The sun is higher. The snow does melt in between snow storms. Meanwhile the daffodils and tulips are fully flowering you know where. The birds are singing and people start wearing shorts.

By April the snow is pretty much gone here on PEI, but no way, no how does that mean spring has arrived. It's still cold, very cold! Some heady days the temperature rises but the fields are still brown and not a green leaf is to be seen. Okay, I lie. Some early bushes have started to sprout a leaf here and there.

We moved to PEI from BC and arrived on May 8th. We're talking *May* here, and I said to my husband, "Where are the leaves on the trees? Why are there no leaves on the trees? And where is the *green*?"

By the time June rolls around most of the trees are in leaf and the grass is greening up but we're not talking balmy temperatures yet. It is *warmish*. There is a reason why the tourist season here officially starts in July! So for maybe one or two glorious weeks, yes it does feel like spring but hey, look, it's June 21st. Spring is over, folks!

An Island Reverie

Sky above.
Water beside.
Red dirt beneath.
Think nothing thoughts.

Ducks mutter to themselves in the reeds.
A splash of red against coal-black wing;
a blackbird clings to a bulrush.
Two Canada geese flap across my horizon.
Nasal honks resonate.

One frog peeps, then two, then one thousand.

I cannot hear my nothing thoughts.
Dogs shift restlessly.
Shush, I say.
Lie still and listen.

I close my eyes, I see nothing.
I open my eyes, I see the whole universe.

VOICES

Winter Storms

I'm always amazed that a world still exists after a winter storm has hit. When the winds finally ease, and the curtain of snow finally lifts and I can see—I can see!—the neighbours' houses at last, I feel the most immense relief.

The barn will still be standing, always a good thing. I'll scan its roof. So far, so good. No trees have fallen where they shouldn't have such as on the house or the car or the tractor! Garbage cans are still outside the door. Usually.

It seems after the nastiest storms the sun makes an extra special appearance. It shines so brightly, illuminating the already dazzling snow-covered fields. The blue sky has nary a cloud, as if to lull me into thinking it will never storm again.

I wish!

I've come to know and dread the winter storm warning here on PEI. I know the drill.

Pick up any loose junk outside. Check.

Firewood in (3 days worth, just in case). Check.

Water buckets filled should the power go out. Check. This entails mega buckets for the livestock, several buckets for the toilet inside, all cat/dog water dishes filled and several containers of drinking water. Have I missed anything?

Batteries for flashlights charged. Check.

Battery-charged reading light ready. Check.

Phone calls made to all my friends. Check. This is a necessity as we must compare various weather forecasts and generally complain and in my case freak out about said impending storm.

Phone calls made to family on Vancouver Island. Check. (see above, but mostly just to complain and threaten to move back to Vancouver Island!)

I think that list about covers everything.

Thank goodness for wood stoves. When the power goes out we still have heat and by golly, I can cook on it if need be. For sure, the first thing we do when the lights go out is put a kettle on for some tea!

What I really hate about these storms is that they're so often unannounced. I'll look at the forecast one morning, see five days of relative inactivity on the weather front, feel all happy, and then BAM! my girlfriend is calling me and saying, "Have you *seen* the forecast?"

Say what?

So I'll check the weather web site and there it is. The dreaded red bar scrolling across the top of the page.

Winter storm alert.

Winter storm warning.

Blizzard alert.

Blizzard on the way!

Oh no!

VOICES

If You Need Any Help Just Call!

One aspect of living on PEI that never ceases to amaze me is the kindness of people. When we first moved to our twenty-five acres, complete strangers would drive up and introduce themselves. And offer their help. They didn't necessarily specify what kind of help. Just a helping hand if we were in need.

One such person is Farmer J. This man has been incredibly helpful and generous since day one. He's given us hay, straw, oats and livestock! He lets us use his big tractor. He ploughs our fields. In return, my husband will trim the hooves of Farmer J.'s sheep and goat, castrate sundry livestock and help with the chores. Not because Farmer J. expects it but because my husband enjoys his company. And I send over baking whenever I can!

One memorable day, during a raging blizzard, I heard a knock on the door. What the heck? I opened it to see my older neighbour standing there. She'd walked over in a near white-out! Her reason?

"I just wanted to be sure you were ok," she said.

There is one young woman who shears our sheep. She lives about an hour away. We've only met a few times...when she's sheared our sheep! My husband was away once when one of our ewes became very lame. I couldn't handle her on my own. I could have called Farmer J. but he's done so much for us and I didn't want

Kim Smith: If You Need Any Help Just Call!

to subject him to wrangling a 120-pound ewe. So I messaged Alice and asked her for help. Despite her crazy busy life she made the time to drive to our farm, wrestle the ewe down, medicate her foot and give her a shot of antibiotics. And then refused any money. But the ewe needed a second treatment a few days later and Alice gladly drove all the way out again. This time I made her take some money!

Other friends, a couple who rescue any animals in need, took care of our horses for us once (long story!) and I know if I ever need their help, they will make the trip. "Just call us, any time! Even in the middle of the night!"

We can rely on our neighbours for help when needed. I take great comfort knowing they are close by. Many is the time my husband has needed a hand lifting or moving some heavy item and the local guys are happy to pop by, even after a long day at work.

One of the most common phrases, I swear, that has been uttered to us is, "If you need any help, just call."

VOICES

Karen Stewart

Karen Stewart returned to her Island roots after a thirty-year career in health care, and now resides in 'Montague the Beautiful'. The treasures of the Island fuel this gentle soul's ever evolving spirituality.

She will often remark, "The stars are never obscured by smog here on PEI."

A warm and caring humanitarian, Karen loves to volunteer, paint and write.

Blessed with a special gift of clairvoyance, Karen is a proficient spiritual tarot card reader and has studied numerology for twenty years.

She feels her many dear friends are her spiritual family on this earthly plane.

VOICES

My Eureka Moments

The War Was Over. It was August of 1954 and I was six years old and living in Saint John, New Brunswick with my mother and two sisters. My Dad was returning from his stint in The Korean Conflict, which has since been declared The Korean War. I was very much anticipating his arrival.

The day finally came when the front door flung open to reveal a man wearing an army uniform, a kit bag slung over his shoulder and sporting a red bushy beard. In horror, I burst into tears and blubbered, "Who is this man? He is *not* my Dad."

Karen Stewart

Aside from some black and white photographs revealing a smiling, clean shaven, handsome man in his thirties, I remembered very little about my father. This man then tenderly picked me up, smilingly reassuring me that indeed he was my Dad but that I had been fooled by his bushy red beard. A short while later he reappeared now clean shaven, reminding me of the Dad I had seen in pictures. Immediately, I felt relaxed and happy around him.

Dad opened his kit bag and surprised me with a pair of beautifully hand embroidered silk pajamas. I clearly remember just before I fell asleep wearing my new handsome pajamas that Mom and Dad were standing over my bed. Laughingly, Dad remarked to my Mom "Look at Shorty stretching." Well, I guess I did not stretch quite enough, as sixty years later I am still nicknamed Shorty, much to my chagrin!

The following morning I was in the kitchen with my Mom watching her bake biscuits. Dad cocked his head around the corner saying that he had a special surprise for me after lunch but that I would have to stay inside so as not to spoil the surprise. The wait seemed an eternity until Dad called me outside. To my delight, there was a tent-like structure fashioned from fir tree boughs. I loved it! Excitedly, I went back inside to tell Mom about my little nest. My Mom then carried a hot buttered biscuit and a glass of cold milk to the back yard.

Something was missing though and I scurried inside to spot a small black velvet cushion that I placed inside my cosy abode. I vividly remember sitting cross-legged on the little black cushion, dressed in a pretty pink and white polka-dot dress, sipping my cold milk and nibbling on my hot buttered biscuit feeling very, very loved and happy.

Olivia. There was one little girl, Olivia, whom I was particularly fond of. She had a warm sunny smile with swinging long brown hair. She had an infectious laugh and was fun to be around. We were inseparable and she was my very best friend. We loved to play together with our dolls, skip, play hopscotch and roam the nearby woods where we played tag with the pretty butterflies. One afternoon she came over with her doll pram and invited me to take a peek inside. To my amusement, her pet cat Charlie was dressed in a pink floral doll's dress, a frilly bonnet and was sporting a string of pearls. Charlie had an 'Anywhere but here, get me out of Dodge' expression on his face. Poor Charlie!

The Grim Reaper. While eating supper one evening I heard a blaring horn and screeching brakes. I quickly ran outside noticing neighbours fleeing their homes and running towards a large white transport truck parked on the street. As I neared, I noticed something light coloured laying in front of the truck.

There was screaming and sobbing. As I wriggled through the crowd I could hear a siren in the distance. I looked down and saw what looked like my dear friend Olivia lying asleep on the pavement. She looked so pale and still. I thought to myself, Olivia, don't be so silly, get up. Stop playing tricks.

I heard Olivia's mother screaming, "My little girl is dead."

At the tender age of six, this was my first encounter with death.

I vividly remember sobbing while in my mind trying to grapple with the meaning of death. I kept thinking this was probably just a bad dream. When my crying subsided, I began to realize that I would not be playing with Olivia again. I kept asking "Why? Why? Why?" Could it be that God picks the most beautiful flowers first? I really did not know.

Adieu! Adieu!. Just a week later, Mom and Dad announced to us three girls that we would be moving to Beach Point, Prince Edward Island, a small fishing and farming community at the far southeast corner where Dad was born. Dad was going to try his hand at lobstering. We would be staying with our grandfather until our new home was ready.

I was rather glad to hear this news, as at every turn I was reminded Olivia was gone. I missed her terribly and was lost without her. Several days later we set out on our journey to PEI. While crossing on the ferry, I was mesmerized by the endless expanse of diamond-capped waves and pondering what possibly could be keeping this huge vessel afloat. I was trying hard to not think of little Olivia's untimely passing, but despite my attempts any joy I felt was eclipsed. Eventually, Dad pointed out PEI, a small strip of red cliffs on the horizon.

I've Arrived. It was dark when we finally arrived at my grandfather's. The large country kitchen was dimly lit with oil lamps. Grandfather, a small balding man in his seventies smiled warmly.

My grandmother passed at age fifty-seven. Six months prior her twenty-year-old son Fred was killed in action while serving in World War II. Three other sons, including my Dad, fortunately returned. Grandmother gave birth to her last child, a son, in 1927 at the age of forty. For many years after that, she had been very ill, most likely as a result of a stroke, although the exact cause was not determined. Apparently she suffered from a weakened physical state requiring lots of bed rest. Parenting of the two younger children in particular was further complicated by the Great Depression. My grandparents raised nine children, the last of whom passed away in 2012.

Valentine sent from Dad while in Korea

The Old Farmhouse. The next morning while eating my breakfast, I gazed curiously about the kitchen. An old dinosaur of a wood stove dominated, its pipes snaking up the wall, offering the sole source of heat to the entire house. The top part of the stove housed a warming oven. A built-in water tank supplied hot water, providing the voraciously hungry stove was fed often. A pair of very old hand-painted oil lamps with soot blackened globes sat on a shelf. An old mantle clock ticked tirelessly. Frayed and faded curtains fluttered in the breeze from unscreened windows. A grotesque blackened fly sticker hung from the ceiling boldly displaying its trophies.

The nearby attached porch housed a tall floor pump offering the only source of water. A woodbox sat inside the porch door. I noticed a large metal ring bolted to the floor. Grandfather sensing my curiosity, pulled hard on the ring lifting up a heavy wooden hatch. I gingerly tip-toed closer and with my heart pounding loudly looked down to see a red clay cellar. What a relief! I could not help think about the fate of the flies. I glimpsed at a faded hand-hooked floor mat displaying a bouquet of flowers at its centre and wondered if my grandmother had crafted it many years ago.

Exploring. By this time I was anxious to go outside to see tiny sparkling diamonds melting in the morning sun. Summer was ripe. Wild pink roses and climbing white morning glories emitted the sweetest fragrance only Mother Nature could birth. Grandfather's house was in keeping with the times, a two-story wooden structure with a center hall plan.

The old barn was home to several horses and cows. I climbed the steps to the hayloft. The grimy window did not diminish the breathtaking view of the vast blue water, red shoreline and fluffy white clouds pasted on a painfully blue sky. I was awestruck!

I eagerly explored the farm yard only to discover one delight after another. A rooster crowed and strutted about the noisy hen coop. I gathered up some still warm eggs from the nests and brought them to the kitchen.

Oysters Anyone?. I noticed my grandfather sitting on the back doorstep shucking an oyster and swallowing its raw and slimy contents. My eyes opened wide in disgust! Surely, I must have turned fifty shades of green as I politely declined his offer to sample an oyster. Ugh!

Busy. Busy. Busy. Mom and Dad were roll-up your sleeve people. Mom was busily housecleaning. Dad was cutting the weed-infested long grass with a sickle. Grandfather spent a lot of time tending to his prize-winning vegetable garden across the red dirt road. The old farmstead was beginning to respond to their tender loving care.

The Old Apple Tree. The massive old apple tree extended a warm welcome to an array of warbling birds to build their nests and raise their families. The gnarled trunk bore battle scars of carved initials and names. W.G.S., April 10, 1926, my Dad's initials, made my eyes pop! Broken and fractured limbs revealed the ravages of Mother Nature and Father Time. Sun-ripened red apples colourfully decorated the sprawling branches. Tiny pale blue broken eggshells lay on the grass, remnants of a baby robin's debut. The old tree offered further blessings when Dad surprised me by hanging a swing for me. How I loved to swing. Cares were forgotten. A feeling of euphoria flooded over me as I soared higher and higher.

Stewart's Creek. The next day was warm and breezy. I wanted to explore some of the neighbourhood. I went to the bottom of the hill to Stewart's Creek on the north side. The large creek was fed by the saltwater from the strait beyond. I remember removing my shoes and anklets and wading in the warm salty water with the sun warm on my face. Gulls lazily soared above. I noticed a pair of long-legged cranes eyeing their breakfast. Numerous tiny wee gudgeons gently nudged and caressed my ankles and legs. I felt part of this tranquil scene. To this very day, many years later, I can visualize in my mind the memory of this little piece of heaven. Immediately I am soothed and calmed. Stewart's Creek became a favorite haunt for me!

The Picnic. One day, we picnicked on the beach. The weather was sunny and quite warm. The old Beach Point Light House was ushering boats safely into harbour. Swallows swooped down from their nests in the lofty red cliffs. Squawking seagulls were perched on red sandstone rocks waiting for someone to discard a tasty morsel. The salt water was as warm as fresh milk. Dancing plovers claimed a sandbar as their stage. A seal bobbed its head and teasingly barked at a distance. Rolling gentle waves caressed the shore.

We ate cucumber sandwiches, potato salad, lemonade and Mom's scrumptious wild raspberry coconut tarts. Later, I wandered along the beach. I saw some sparkling clear spring water trickling down from a red-clay cliff. I was thirsty and cupped my hands under the flow of cold water and drank deeply.

My curiosity was aroused when I eyed pretty coloured rocks

strewn about. There was one particular stone that made my eyes pop in amazement as it sparkled in the sunlight. I was so sure I had struck gold that I scooped it up and ran down the beach to share my fantastic find with my family. I was excitedly explaining to Mom and Dad that the shiny gold flakes must indeed be gold and worth a fortune when I noticed Mom putting her hand over her mouth to conceal her mirth. Dad saw my obvious disappointment and explained that a ship carrying a cargo of rocks had gone off course and went aground many years ago. Mom said it was only Fool's Gold. Well I sure was fooled!

The sun was slowly sinking and it was time to pack up and go home. I did not want the day to end but Mom said we would come back again.

Awed. After supper, I went outside to swing. Beyond this space, to the west, the vibrant red sunset graced a long row of spruce trees. I was still on cloud nine reliving my perfect day. I gave extra thanks to God for weaving such a magnificent tapestry. Surely He must have devoted some extra attention to creating the Island. I did not need toys to amuse me as my joy was fueled by the delights of the Island. This magical playground offered adventure at every turn.

Edna. On Saturday, September 11th, 1954 I was awakened by a loud hammering coming from outside. I was curious and dashed downstairs. I asked Mom what all the commotion was about. She calmly explained that the men of the community were boarding up windows and securing boats as a storm might be headed our way. Mom tried to reassure me that this was a precautionary measure and not to be overly concerned and that perhaps we would be spared. Despite Mom's comforting words, I still felt antsy. It was overcast and unusually balmy. I felt an uneasiness when I looked at the sky.

Night finally came and I was sent off to bed. I was tossing and turning until sleep eventually overcame me. Then a thunderous clap jolted me and I shot up in bed like a rocket. Rain pelted the roof and window panes. It was pitch black except when the room was illuminated by a powerful flash of lightning. I could hear a loud roaring and I vividly remember the old house shaking. There was a loud bang as if a car had rammed into the west side of the house. My heart was in my throat. My words were frozen when I attempted to call out to Mom. Suddenly, my Mom's arms enveloped me and I felt safe once more.

By morning the storm was abating somewhat. Apparently we were hit hard by Hurricane Edna, a powerfully devastating storm. Gale force winds topped eighty miles per hour (roughly 128 k.p.h.), and trees were uprooted or broken off. Windows were shattered. It was reported by the newspaper that a heavy fishing boat sitting in a field was moved some forty feet by fierce winds. A brown-coloured blight covered deciduous trees, plants, fruits, flowers and vegetables probably due to the driving salt sea spray blowing inland from the strait.

Mom insisted that we not go outside until the winds had fully subsided. I remember gingerly walking through the soggy wet grass to the backyard. There were small pond sized mud puddles. I stared in shocked disbelief when I saw my precious apple tree split from top to bottom. Bruised and brown-coloured apples were strewn all about. My swing was a tangled mess on the soggy grass. Swollen waterlogged morning glories and wild pink roses lay limp on the wet grass with only a hint of yesterday's beauty. My little piece of paradise was lost. I sobbed as if my heart would break.

Pain. The Great Teacher. Again, I found myself asking, "Why? Why? Why?"

Magically, a warm ray of sunshine shone brightly and lit up my dreary day. I felt a whispersoft touch on my hand and to my amazement a spectacular monarch butterfly fluttered its wings. My thoughts instantly turned to little Olivia. I knew then in my heart that she had been transformed into spirit form as the beautiful butterfly had been by God. I still am reminded that Olivia is with me offering faith, hope, guidance and courage to walk in love on my earthly journey. I realized God loved me and had kept my family and me safe during the hurricane. God would restore my earthly home back to its former beauty.

Hey, I'm Home. Dad would often speak of having 'salt in his blood' and that he felt driven to return home to the red shores of Prince Edward Island. I now know what Dad meant by this as I too have returned after thirty-seven years of 'living away'. And would you believe it, within two weeks of my arrival in September 2003, Hurricane Juan struck with a vengeance. The exact scenario played itself out again in a way reminiscent of my maiden voyage to PEI at age six. Now, sixty years later any hint of an approaching hurricane puts me on high alert. Despite this, it would take more than a hurricane to uproot me again. I'm here to stay!

Salt in the blood is a highly contagious malady resistant to any known medical intervention. Symptoms include an intense longing, accompanied by restlessness and a vague sense of feeling orphaned. Some folks however, have experienced tremendous relief when they pulled up stakes and fled to PEI post-haste. Curiously, their symptoms magically disappeared. Just ask a dear friend of mine *from away* who came to visit me for a couple of weeks last spring. She too fell madly in love with the Island. When she left, she came down with a very severe case of salt in the blood. Since then, she has been transplanted to the red shores of PEI and is thriving.

So if you come for a visit, and I hope you do, don't be surprised when you leave if you too begin to exhibit symptoms of salt in the blood. Don't waste precious time seeking a cure *from away*. Instead, come home!

Linda Stewart

I don't recall anything quite so thrilling as seeing my first piece published. It was a handwritten essay, *'Simple Country Pleasure'* and I thought it a really daring thing to do to submit it to *Common Ground* magazine in the summer of 1990, but it appeared in their October issue and so began my writing career. Since then, my work has appeared in other island publications, as well as a number of Canadian and US magazines and literary journals.

I love the arts and one of my favourite compliments was being told that I have a 'very artistic air'! My fiddling and acting are two more passions of my life. Both are too much fun! Growing up in rural PEI has had a profound effect on me and I believe contributed greatly to my writerly soul. I spent my childhood in a tiny, tucked-away community called Iris, and the rest of my life has been spent in Wood Islands, a lovely farming and fishing community along the southeastern shores of PEI.

My faith is such an ingrained facet of my being that I am often asked about a poem that I've written, "Is that about God?" It might be about chocolate but somehow they still wonder if it is spiritual.

I feel the word 'hobby', especially in regards to my writing, demeans the arts. Another pleasantry which I dislike is 'well, it's good pastime for you!'. On the other hand, one of my favourite quotes is from Thomas Kincaid: *"How will you use the talents within you? Will you belittle the gifts you've been given, regarding them as "frivolous" and relegating them to an obscure corner of your life? Or will you use them to uplift and inspire others, by infusing everything you do with meaning and purpose?"*

VOICES

Downsized

*I loved the very ground of the place
the generational farm house
Green Gables look-a-like
our Eden with the roses climbing the veranda
where little boys grew up
grandfathers held court
beloved dogs chased balls
and cats...
where each Springtime
I waited and watched
for my faithful ones
the crocuses, forget-me-nots,
lily of the valley, tulips, roses
and more...
Here in this idyllic piece of islandness
I found poetry, music, and light.*

*My Victorian masterpiece belongs to others now
and goes on being loved, being charming, being a haven.
But will it not always be the poet's house?
Eden and I are inseparable.
It lives and still feels my footsteps
around the circular lane.
The upstairs bedroom
must still ring from the strains of my violin.
In the corner of the living room
there must still be tap-tapping of poems
spilling, tumbling, on to white paper.
The veranda must remember how often I sat there
soaking in the beauty of the garden.*

This Place

*A poetic atmosphere
permeates this place
where the ordinary
and the sublime unite
and life flows on
in steady rhythm
day to day
hour by hour.
Time whispers its quiet passing
in the hands of a clock
on a wall.
It promises nothing
except echoes that will ring
through the heart of this place
in far off years to come.
As the winds blow the maples
and Autumn leaves fall
as the snow gently drifts
to the cold hard earth
as April rains pour down
and the grass begins to green
and the roses
from their buds burst forth
with sweet fragrance to instill
the pervading atmosphere of this place
will always be
an ethereally beautiful
and poetic one.*

Linda Stewart: Watercolour Pastels

Watercolour Pastels

Eerie cries of seals offshore...
Stillness.
The quiet of saltwater welting,
sinking, lapping over
claws of gulls standing
silently by the tide's edge.
Fresh western breeze...
a welcome coolness against
the sun's heat.
Blue, blue sky...
white clouds scattered, feathered
offers of beauty
remembered in childhood
for those who care to look up.
Marine life crackles underfoot.
Across the shore, a lighthouse.
A ferryboat leaves the dock.
Halcyon scenes in watercolour pastels...

From Original oil painting by Nancy Perkins

VOICES

Light and Stardust

One day...
I will only haunt
the red mud lanes
and the nearby shores
like a film of light and stardust
my presence will linger...
The poet in me
will always be here.
I will whisper through the trees
on quiet Autumn evenings
and peer through the stars
on calm Winter nights.
My skirts will brush you
ever-so-slightly
on promising spring twilights
and summer sunsets will weep
as I gaze through mists of love
on Northumberland waves
where the gulls and I
made our peace.
I will kiss you while you sleep
and you will know my perfume
when you wake....

My Island

The mystical magical
shades of life
escape not my attention
in these island shores
where the cliffs are red
the gulls loud
and the sea
a salty rolling blue.
I am alone on this island
It belongs only to me
because this island lives in my heart
in a place no other soul
has been able to reach.
The loneliness of the island
is a friend in and of itself
understanding me too well
and the winds that sashay
across its wide open expanses
seduces me into fancying that
herein lies eternity
where changes never occur
and where time does not exist.
I want my island
to stay the island of long ago
where old buckets
hang by farm house gates
and wagons sit isolated
in fields of golden hay
and dusty clay roads
wind through hills and valleys
in silence and solitude.
This is my island
my mystical magical eternal island.

VOICES

The Farmers Market

My visits to the Charlottetown Farmers Market on Saturday mornings are always a treat. Many facets of the market feed my soul, as well as my body and spirit. The welcoming aroma of fresh ground, artisan brewed coffee that greets me when I walk through the door. The bustling crowd and happy noise. The proud vendors and their homegrown, homemade wares and the often ethnic food such as a delicious falafel sandwich I choose for my lunch.

While I eat my lunch at one of the big, old wooden picnic tables in the dining section a pleasant French Canadian man turns out to be a good conversationalist. His son who later joins us chats a bit, too. We talk about why we love the market. We talk about Quebec where they are originally from and we talk about Old Quebec City which I enjoyed visiting a few years ago and which happened to be on my travel bucket list. We are strangers being kind, open, friends… for a little while.

And who would have thought that a farmers market would be the happenin' place to be, but it is a veritable Who's Who of Prince Edward Island. You see local celebrities out for their fresh, organic veggies. The vendors have practically become celebrities and the cool, hip crowd who frequent the market, if not real celebrities, look like celebs. It is, after all, an artistic, down-to-earth-yet-sophisticated environment.

Favourite purchases at the market include homemade pickles and jam, artisan breads and coffee, fresh flower bouquets, locally produced honey and vegetables, handmade soaps, and farm fresh eggs. It is important for me to purchase eggs that were laid by chickens that get to scratch around in the yard as opposed to being kept in a cage all day.

As well as real food, locally sourced and humanely produced, the farmers market provides community. It is a place where we are shoulder to shoulder, united in our appreciation for our roots that are embedded deep in our red soil. For a little while, on Saturday mornings, we are all rural and we are all neighbours.

VOICES

Farm Living

(Inspired by the farm of Farrell & Kate Reeves, Freetown, PEI)

*Farm living, early rising
cows grazing, dogs barking
rooster crowing, chores to tend
eggs to gather*

*Landscape beauty
clear blue sky
tractor humming
soil ploughed even*

*Apple pie cooling
fresh laundry on the line
clean aprons, flour on noses
potted plants on the sill*

*Harvest time
gardens to weed, produce to sell
canning and preserving
children playing*

*Cold weather preparations
hard work and sweat
helpful friends and neighbours
round the kitchen table*

This is farm living.

A Memorable Meal

I felt part of a Norman Rockwell painting.
We tried a new restaurant outside town.
I had a sense of belonging to a select circle,
a family circle.

We were seated in a narrow, intimate room.
In one corner, a gent reading The Guardian newspaper
occupied a small table for two;
a family of three—father, mother, teenage son—
looked like they just stepped off the farm
to grab a bite out;
just arm's length away from us
an elderly man seemed content with his solitary meal;
behind our table, another couple dining out,
and next to them, a burly truck driver fuelling up
for the road with a hefty helping of meat & potatoes.

The farm family bowed their heads. It was a touching moment.
The atmosphere was quiet, almost rarified.
Our food arrived, a generous helping of homestyle fare.
I had an unusual feeling that all of us,
in that room, for that hour, were at home.

VOICES

Perfect Silence

*I am listening to the silence.
But it is not perfect silence.
There is the ticking of the clock,
the crackling of the wood,
the sigh of the dog
as he plops down on the floor,
and an incessant hum, somewhere,
in the airwaves?
Outside the wind is blowing.
The surf is loud upon the shore
and hundreds of geese
in nearby fields
strike up a chorus.
Perfect silence
is hard to find.*

God Sounds

*This place affords me solitude
with only the lapping waves
the cry of gulls
the flapping wings
of a blue heron
to break the silence.
I write with the simplicity
of my surroundings*

No one disturbs me here

*I wish
that I could stay
and be just me
listening to God-sounds*

www.ingramcontent.com/pod-product-compliance
Lightning Source LLC
Chambersburg PA
CBHW071923290426
44110CB00013B/1458